Table of Contents

ADULT LITERACY HANDBOOK FOR STUDENTS AND TUTORS

SEVENTH EDITION

Anita H. Pomerance, Ph.D
Editor

Published and produced by:

 **Center for Literacy**
Learning for Life

Center for Literacy, Inc.
636 S. 48th Street
Philadelphia, PA 19143

JoAnn Weinberger, President/Executive Director

Dedicated to the thousands of volunteer tutors and adult learners who over the years have worked together to meet the learners' literacy goals. Without them, this handbook would never have been created.

ISBN 0-9785469-0-3

Printed in the U. S. A.

Acknowledgements

This book, the Adult Literacy Handbook for Tutors and Students, is based on a combination of current research and the Center for Literacy's (CFL) 38 years of experience in teaching adult students and training volunteers. The process in creating this revised edition took three years and involved many contributors.

The first person we would like to thank is Judi Taylor-Dunn, the Director of Education Services at the Center for Literacy. She managed the process of the development of the handbook including insuring the content is research-based and developing the bibliography.

We also appreciate the contributions made by CFL's adult literacy professionals including: Corey Abbott, Scott Bostwick, Paul Bryson, Vann Delaine, Mark Edmonds, Elaine Green, Ron Hopkins, Nicole Jackson, Katherine Stutzman, and Mike Vail. We especially thank those staff members who authored sections of the manual; Stephanie Korber who wrote the text on learning disabilities found throughout the manual and Don Nix who wrote the chapter on technology.

We received valuable assistance and input from Anita Pomerance, the original author of previous editions and the lead editor of this edition. Others who provided editorial suggestions on content and format were Alisa Belzer and Lynda Ginsberg from the Graduate School of Education at Rutgers, the State University of New Jersey. Alisa Belzer's expertise in adult literacy, volunteer tutoring and adult reading development were called upon to help us articulate our philosophical view of how to best teach reading and writing. Lynda Ginsberg provided the same guidance in the area of numeracy. We sincerely appreciate the time and effort that they spent on working with us to make this an educationally sound product.

Many of the activities and ideas in this book were in previous editions created by former CFL staff members. We acknowledge their contributions, which helped shape who CFL is today. Those contributors were Joan Barasovska, Alisa Belzer, Rose Brandt, Maria Bottiglieri, Sandra Choukoun, Marlyn DeWitt, Becky Eno, Dianna Gray, Sandy Harrill, Martha Lane, Judi Lashoff, Bridget Joan Martin, Rachel Martin, Kate McGeever, Jane McGovern, Martha Merson, Sue Newman, Shana Nixon, Lucy Park, Jamie Preston, Camille Realo, Irene Schauer, Catherine DeLong Smith, Jeanne Smith, Dan Smythe, Emma Tramble, Marie Vannozzi, Yvette Walls, Richard Wells, Elizabeth White and Velma Wood.

We also thank Pamela Spencer for using her excellent word processing skills to format each chapter, David Rosen for reviewing our final draft and writing the introduction, and Rhona Candeloro for graphic design.

Finally, a special 'thank you' to JoAnn Weinberger, President/Executive Director of the Center for Literacy whose vision and leadership inspired all of us to work together to complete this project.

Introduction to CFL Tutor Handbook

The word tutor, which most Americans think of as someone who provides one-on-one direct instruction, does not adequately describe the range of critical roles for one who helps an adult learn to read, write and compute. Other words that could broaden our understanding, and which you will see featured here, include: guide, supporter, encourager, resource, partner and co-explorer.

As a literacy tutor, you may already read and write well; you may be an expert reader or writer. But you may be a novice as a guide through the process of learning to read and write as an adult. As an adult learner, you may not yet read or write English well, but you are an expert in surviving in the world without being able to read and write in English, but with other skills for gaining useful knowledge, such as active listening, remembering, and finely sharpened critical thinking. You may be an excellent reader or writer of other languages. And you are an expert on what learning strategies do and don't work – for you. You are an expert in knowing what you want or need to read or write, or in how you want to use mathematics. Together, as a tutor-learner partnership, you will both learn about how someone in the United States becomes literate, and competent and comfortable with numbers and computers, as an adult. This handbook will help you to do that.

Although the content of the handbook has grown out of the years of experience of tutor preparation at one program, the Center for Literacy in Philadelphia, it can be applied at literacy programs anywhere in North America, and perhaps beyond. It is based on deep knowledge of adult learners and of the range of kinds of people who make good volunteer tutors. It was designed in an urban center but it should also be useful in a rural setting, for people tutoring one-on-one, and in small groups, and also for those who provide help which is supplemental to classroom instruction.

What is unique about this handbook, and the Center for Literacy approach, however, is not wisdom and common sense, both of which this has in abundance; not its practical tutor and learner resources, of which there are plenty; not that it recommends a balanced approach to teaching reading and writing, which it does; not that it rightly includes numeracy and computer skills; but rather its view of learners and tutors as a team, as collaborators. It is a manual which helps and respects both tutor and learner, and which draws on the tutor's basic skills navigating expertise, while keeping the adult learner in the driver's seat.

David J. Rosen, Ed.D.
Senior Associate
Newsome Associates
August 4, 2005

Chapter 1

Overview of Adult Literacy Tutoring

The purpose of this chapter is to provide information which will serve as background for the teaching strategies described later in the book. We describe the history and structure of the Center for Literacy, whose students, tutors, and staff provide the experience upon which this handbook is based. We explain how its present training developed. We also describe the participants in literacy training: the life situations, motives, and roles of literacy students and tutors. Finally, we present the characteristics of different grouping arrangements.

I. CENTER FOR LITERACY (CFL)

A. Background

The Center for Literacy is the nation's largest community-based, nonprofit adult literacy agency. Its mission is: **"To provide a range of literacy services, including reading, writing, math, life and work skills, to help a diverse population of learners meet their needs and achieve their personal and employment-related goals."** Since 1968, it has provided adult basic and literacy education throughout the Philadelphia area to adults who want to improve their reading, writing, math, and English language skills to function more effectively in the family, workplace, and community. Tutoring is only one of the services provided by the Center for Literacy, which currently serves nearly 5,000 adult learners, with a paid staff of more than 80, and more than 275 volunteer tutors.

B. The Student-Tutor Orientation

Building upon 38 years of tutor training experience, CFL has developed its own approach to preparing volunteers for tutoring. It currently provides several eight-hour, three-session tutor trainings per month in different parts of Philadelphia and Delaware Counties.

In 1989, Center for Literacy staff members designed and began using the Student-Tutor Orientation, an innovative training which provided hands-on experience by including learners as well as prospective tutors. It consists of three sessions covering a total of eight hours. The first session of the training is for tutors only because they take part in activities that sensitize them to the learner's point of view and do some activities that require proficient reading.

Learners participate in the last two sessions, where they are paired with tutors. Having learners participating gives the tutors an opportunity for hands-on experience, and it also establishes the partnership between learners and tutors. If personalities or learning and teaching styles are incompatible, there is always the possibility of trying a different match. Coming to these training sessions with their tutors benefits the learners because adult learners do best when they participate in planning their own instruction. To do so, they need to know the same things about reading, writing, and adult learning as the tutors.

The training is based on the belief that learning should occur by hearing about, observing, and then doing the skill to be learned, followed by feedback from experienced observers. Therefore, tutors and students come together to the second and third sessions to hear about learning strategies, see them modeled, and try them out, with the opportunity to ask questions and get guidance from CFL staff.

Occasionally, when it would be difficult to arrange for students to come, CFL has trainings for tutors only. For example, such trainings are scheduled for federal employees with tight security regulations or for staff of one corporation who plan to tutor in different sections of the city.

II. THE LITERACY PARTNERS

A. The Learners

1. Who are the literacy learners? What they tell us.

The following excerpts come from interviews and written records of adult learners describing early experiences with learning to read and write, as well as difficulties that they have faced due to limits in basic skills.

First Interview: (male learner)

Interviewer: So tell me, about how far did you go in school?

Learner: Well, to be honest, I actually finished school. But, as you know, sometimes you're not fully prepared or somehow you didn't go the route that you should have went. Sometimes maybe you're the type of person that just doesn't comprehend like others. I think that was part of my problem…comprehension and spelling and those types of things.

Interviewer: Do you think your teachers knew that you were having some problems with comprehension in school?

Learner: Well I think that some of them might have knew I was having some problems, but by the same token, I did fairly well in school. But, I was a 24-7 type of guy…I couldn't let up. Some could study in an hour or so and be outside playing. If I were going to get anything out of it, I had to put 4-5 hours into studying.

Interviewer: You have a high school diploma. What made you decide to come back to school?

Learner: You know, just having a piece of paper without being equipped is not enough.

Interviewer: How did you know that you weren't equipped? What did you want to do, that you felt you weren't able to do?

Learner: Um…let's just say, writing checks…writing the figures out…writing the names on the checks. Sometimes it was tough spelling the words. So…my spelling has always been a problem. That is a major reason why I'm here.

Interviewer: Do you think this has impacted your work life?

Learner: I have a feeling that some jobs I would have gone after, I didn't because of my educational level. Because some of the applications are a little more difficult than others, so that's one thing that kept me back.

Interviewer: What are you doing now?

Learner: Right now I'm not working, but when I was working, I worked for a company that supplied products to steel companies. Our product insulated and deoxidized the steel. They closed the company this year. This is the time in my life to readjust my life…

Second Interview: (female learner)

Interviewer: While going to school, did you have problems with reading?

Learner: I started having problems when I got to the third grade. I was in LD (learning disabilities) class third grade through the seventh…then I took a test and I was in regular classes. I had a lot of teachers that liked me. I did things for them and they let me pass.

Interviewer: What was it like in the early grades? You said you started having trouble in third grade. How did it feel for you in class at that time?

Learner: I thought I was doing okay. I really did. Then when I got in special education class… I was really mad about it. I didn't think I should've been in that room because kids is acting up. I think if you're slow and you have kids acting up, they should be in another classroom.

Interviewer: How do you use reading and writing in your daily life?

Learner: I don't write anything. I just really started understanding signs, reading the paper...I be trying to read the Bible...

Excerpts from Writings:

Writing from female learner, ESL

> *I'm from Ivory Coast, a small country in West Africa. I'm fifty-five years old. I have three children. They live in Abidjan, the capital. Before I came to the USA, I was teaching in elementary school. I didn't earn a lot of money, but the work was easy. Here the work is hard. I work in two different restaurants. I leave my home in morning and come back at midnight.*

> *I start at 9 a.m. at the first restaurant and finish at 5 p.m. I have to sweep and clean bathrooms and prepare the kitchen before the cooks start their work. I never get a rest. I do this and that all day. Then I run to the second restaurant and do the same thing until midnight. It's not easy for me. I have another difficulty – the language. I don't speak English very well. I can't tell my problems to my chefs and patrons. Even in the bus and trains I don't like it if anyone asks me about something.*

As these stories reveal, some of the reasons adults did not learn to read and write include being labeled unable to learn, unhelpful placement in special education classes, family problems, illness, frequent moving, and perceptions of school as a place where they would be laughed at. Issues related to poverty, violence, and addictions have also proven to be barriers to literacy, as have language challenges for non-native speakers of English.

What we know about literacy learners: Literacy learners are competent adults. Many are skilled workers and/or active community members. Most learners do read and write to some extent; few are totally unable to read and write. Literacy learners generally are working or trying to, and have had some experience with the educational system. At the Center for Literacy, for example, learners range in age from sixteen to their seventies, with the majority in their thirties or forties. The majority have completed some high school. There tend to be more women in classes, and more men in tutoring.

2. What is the role of the adult learner?

The Center for Literacy believes in collaborative and student-centered learning. That is, we believe in putting adult learners in control of their own learning. Learners and tutors are encouraged to work collaboratively in planning lessons and choosing materials. Research has shown that adults learn faster when lessons are based on their own goals and needs. Learners usually decide to work with a range of materials and activities to meet goals which might include reading the newspaper or Bible, completing job applications, managing their finances, or attaining a driver's license.

The adult learner should have a role as a partner in the process of learning. This partnership is an active one, with the contribution of the learner being a key component. The CFL has observed that this partnership is empowering to the learner. An empowered learner is more likely to persevere in setting and achieving his or her personal and academic goals.

B. The Tutors

1. Who are the literacy tutors? What they tell us.

Literacy tutors give personal reasons for wanting to tutor adults in literacy. Many say that they love to read, and they want to share that pleasure with another person. Some say they always wanted a chance to try teaching, while others are ex-teachers who miss their old jobs. Some people say they have time on their hands and want to do something interesting. Other people work in a closed environment all day and want to work with people outside of the home. Yet others have overcome educational or personal problems themselves and want to help others to do the same thing. There are also immigrants who had to achieve English language literacy and are passionate about helping other people to accomplish this. Some tutors speak of wanting to "give back to the community" the good things that they have gained from it in their own lives.

Excerpts from Interviews with Tutors:

Interviewer: Why did you become a literacy tutor?

Tutor 1: I became a tutor because I can't imagine anyone going through life without being able to read and write. I've found out about the world and myself through reading, and when I've gone through a dark night of the soul, it's been solace.

I have been able to express myself in writing as I never could in conversation. Montaigne once marveled at the fact that he could express the intimate details of his life in print that he could never reveal to his closest friend. I feel the same way.

Tutor 2: My wife was a tutor before me. She worked with prison inmates. At that time, it really struck me how important reading and writing were. I asked myself what chance these people had in rebuilding their lives if they couldn't read. I made the decision to become a tutor. I've been paired with several learners, including a couple of immigrants. It was plain to see how hard it was for them to be successful here with limited speaking and literacy ability. I found that one of my learners really lacked confidence. As our partnership developed, she became more self-assured with me and then with other people. She's moved on to studying for a professional degree now. I've also learned a lot.

What we know about literacy tutors: As a group, literacy tutors resemble the literacy learners in many ways. They range in age from high school seniors of seventeen to people in their seventies. They reflect the ethnic makeup of their own neighborhoods where they usually tutor. Some tutors do their tutoring as part of college courses, and some are recruited on the job. The majority are employed and tutor during their lunch hour or after work. They usually share enthusiasm for meeting and helping new people.

2. What is the role of the literacy tutor?

In addition to being a "partner" to a literacy learner, most successful tutors also think of themselves as a "coach" or a "guide." As we have seen, many adult learners have had negative experiences learning as children. Therefore, the tutor should not take on the role of "teacher," one which may evoke the fears, frustrations, and humiliations likely experienced by their literacy partners during their childhoods.

The tutor might serve in the role of helper. The learner may ask for help with a task that needs immediate attention, such as reading a piece of important mail, completing a form, or responding to a letter from a child's teacher. In a case like this,

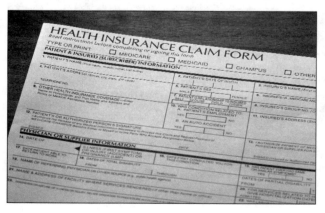

the tutor helps the learner by completing the needed task with her. The learner is helped with the immediate need and begins to work toward performing the task independently.

As instructor, the tutor provides explanations and feedback on the learner's activities. Whatever the specific activity may be, the tutor encourages self-reliance and creates an atmosphere of partnership by doing the following:

- Addressing the learners' immediate and long-term goals.
- Suggesting possible materials and learning strategies.
- Helping find materials.
- Providing help in completing learning activities.
- Helping learners evaluate their own work.
- Supporting the learners' self-esteem by pointing out their successes and abilities and being generally positive and encouraging.
- Realizing that learners may have personal problems which affect the learning process.
- Helping the learners connect with services outside the literacy agency.

It is also important that literacy educators, including tutors, avoid the term "illiterate" because of its demeaning connotation, and because it singles out one characteristic of a complex person as if it is the most important thing about that person. A person who cannot carry a tune, for example, is not belittled for lack of skill in music.

3. Qualifications for tutors

Although people from a wide range of educational backgrounds have been successful tutors, many adult education providers set academic qualifications for their tutors. Even more important than academic level, however, is a sincere desire to help learners achieve their goals. This includes a sense of responsibility toward and a willingness to commit time to the learner, including working outside of the scheduled tutor sessions such as planning for lessons, locating materials, and completing documentation required by the literacy organization.

Tutors can create a positive learning environment by treating learners with respect, and demonstrating the Five C's:

- Cooperation
- Communication
- Creativity
- Compassion
- Committment

C. Grouping for Tutoring

Although tutoring is often thought of as a one-to-one activity, there are a variety of ways to address the varying needs and preferences of learners, tutors, and programs.

1. One-to-one

The traditional model of one tutor working in partnership with one learner has a number of advantages:

For the learners:

- They can focus on specific learning goals or immediate needs for as long as necessary.
- It is a good educational first step; it feels safe.
- It can provide greater personal support from the tutor.
- It may seem less school-like.

For the tutor:

- It can be less intimidating.
- It is easier to predict and to plan the materials and activities.

For learners and tutors:

- Instruction can be tailored to the learner's individual style, interests, and goals.
- It is easier to adapt to unexpected schedule changes.

2. Small groups

There are many advantages to having learners work in small learning groups. Currently, CFL encourages the use of groups of one tutor to about three learners. These are the advantages from the different participants' perspectives:

For learners:

- Seeing that they are not alone with their problem enhances self-esteem, as does the opportunity to utilize personal areas of competency to teach other learners.
- Learners who teach others increase their own understanding.
- Through group interaction, learners have a better

chance of recognizing their own accomplishments.

- Learners are less likely to put off the reading, writing, and math they do at home, as they feel obligated to the group.
- Learners may learn better from others who are nearer their own ability level.

For tutors:

- Working with a variety of learners provides a richer tutoring experience.
- Tutors gain the satisfaction of having a greater impact by serving more learners.
- Tutors enjoy having learners become independent of the tutor by learning from each other.
- Absenteeism does not cancel the session, which is motivating for the tutor.

For both learners and tutors:

- The diversity of individuals and the group interactions are fun to experience.
- Responsibility and accountability are shared.
- Groups have a life and momentum of their own, providing energy to keep them going and increasing the retention of learners in the program.
- Because several people are involved, the learner-tutor relationship is less emotionally intense.

For programs:

- Programs can serve more learners.

3. Larger groups, with more than one tutor

Another possible grouping is to match a larger group of learners with several specialized tutors. Tutors focus on one discipline, such as reading, writing, math, or computers. Learners choose the area in which they participate. An approximate ratio of three learners to one tutor is maintained. Advantages include:

For learners:

- Learners may freely choose different educational activities at different times.
- Moving from station to station increases learning rates among learners with kinesthetic learning styles.

For tutors:

- Tutors are able to focus on subjects in which they feel the most capable.

For learners and tutors:

- An active and interesting learning environment may be formed with lots of possibilities for positive interactions.

Chapter 2

Adult Literacy Learning

I n this chapter, we focus on adult learning. We begin by describing the broad scope of the word "literacy" today. Next, we show some important differences between the learning situation of adults and children, how these differences affect adult learning, and why the most effective relationships between tutors and learners are collaborative with their working together as partners.

We also discuss identifying the learners' goals, including employment and further education, with the help of the Goals Checklist, which is useful for making plans and evaluating progress. Having stated that adults learn and remember best by using the new skills in real situations and by repeated practice, we recommend ways to help learners weave their newly learned activities into their daily routine and make extra time and space for them at home.

I. LITERACY AND ADULT LEARNING

A. What Is Literacy? Isn't Literacy Reading?

In some cases it is, but today's literacy standard is broadening as our society becomes more complex. Literacy means having the basic skills to function in the family, in the community, and on the job. Reading is an important part of this, as it allows us to receive communication in written form. But we also need writing to communicate printed information of everyday life such as a grocery list or a telephone message.

In addition, large segments of the population cannot read or write proficiently in English because they are not proficient in English. For non-native speakers of English, improving in speaking and understanding English may be part of their literacy need.

But is literacy limited to reading, writing, speaking, and listening in English? To be literate, shouldn't a person be able to manage his money, shop for necessities, pay bills, understand a pay stub, file taxes, find an address, or cook from a recipe? These skills require numeracy, the ability to use numbers, for which many adult learners come to literacy providers to improve.

As we become increasingly dependent upon technology, we need at least a basic understanding of computers. Many adult learners are eager to become computer literate, including those who wish to be able to help their children with their schoolwork.

Today's functional standard of literacy will probably be out of date in ten years. Adult literacy tutors and learners need to be open to a wide variety of subjects and methods of study because there are many ways to help learners. As mentioned in Chapter 1, the Center for Literacy's definition of literacy is quite broad: it strives to provide reading, writing, numeracy and English language skills to adults so they can meet their goals and function more effectively in the family, workplace, and community.

B. How Are Adult Learners Different from Children?

Adult learners have different pressures and priorities than children. They may be home-makers and parents, employees with challenging schedules and duties, and may travel long distances to come to sessions. This means they may have difficulty scheduling sessions, be fatigued when they get there, and have difficulty finding time to study outside of the sessions. They need activities which are lively and relevant to their needs.

Adult learners' needs tend to be specific. One learner may need to study reading to get a driver's permit to transport himself to work and his children to school. Another may be interested primarily in balancing her checkbook in order to manage her finances. Such learners may become frustrated if tutoring sessions do not focus on what they see as their area of need, or if they do not see how the material relates to their goal.

Adult learners have more experiences than children. They are familiar with a variety of subjects and like to relate new materials to the information and wisdom which they already possess. Adults like to share their talents and knowledge with others and want to apply new information to their daily lives.

C. How Do Adults Learn?

What do these characteristics tell us? The Center for Literacy has observed that learning is most successful when it is:

- Collaborative: Learners share in the responsibility for their own learning.
- Learner-centered: Adult learners want to have control over deciding what they learn, how they learn it, and when they have learned enough.
- Hands-on: Learning by doing is a natural way to learn, with actual experience doing reading, writing, and numeracy.
- Repeated: Learning should include enough practice as part of the learners' work and leisure for new skills to be remembered. "Use it or lose it."

II. COLLABORATIVE LEARNING

A. How Do Tutors and Learners Achieve Collaborative Learning?

Tutors and adult learners plan the lessons by selecting goals, activities, and materials. They decide how long to work on something, and when they have achieved success. During the opening sessions, especially, they face the challenge of identifying the learner's goals and deciding where to begin.

B. Why Is Collaborative Learning So Important?

The following words of four Center for Literacy learners, as they describe their life and educational goals, show why learners need to be the decision-makers:

"Getting my GED will not only give me pride in knowing that, even after all the years I spent out of school, I could do it. It will also help me on my second goal, which is to get a good job."

"I like to write because it allows me to be creative and imaginative. I get to create characters who I wouldn't mind having as friends. I can model characters after myself, my friends, or family. I like to write because it relaxes me. Mostly I like to write because it gives me a voice. I can say as much or as little as I want without saying a word. Hopefully, one day I will become an accomplished author and then go on to teach others how to write as well."

"The best goal for me is to look forward to helping my son in his reading, math, and writing, and whatever he needs in school and at home. I want to keep his mind on schoolwork and on going to school."

"Math helps me to pay bills, budget money, and make store purchases."

Literacy learners are used to managing their own lives and know their own needs and desires for tutoring. Ideally, they have been able to share them with literacy agency staff during their initial interviews, but if not, they can discuss them with their tutor.

III. WORKING ON LEARNERS' GOALS

Although learners would not enter a literacy program unless they had goals, they may need help in pinning them down clearly enough to know where to begin. CFL has developed a process, including the filling out and discussion of its Goals Checklist, to help the learner and the tutor to clearly identify learners' goals.

A. Long-Term Versus Short-Term Goals

As tutors and learners talk together to discover what the learner really wants, it is helpful to differentiate between long-range plans and short-term goals of doing particular tasks or activities.

- Long-range plans, such as getting into college, require many accomplishments, such as passing tests or interviews or raising money, and often involve greatly increasing proficiency in reading, writing, and numeracy.
- Short-term goals include mastering particular literacy tasks, such as writing postcards, or using specific materials, such as menus, e-mail, children's books, or checkbooks.

1. Why work on short-term goals first?

Although long-range plans must be worked on because they are what brought the learner to the program, there are several reasons for focusing on short-term goals immediately:

- Short-term goals are often steps toward achieving long-range plans.
- Students see progress sooner; adult learners want results immediately, not at some future stage in their lives.
- Learners get the valuable experience of learning by doing.
- Learners see their learning pay off in their personal lives.
- Learners and tutors gain in self-esteem early.
- Learners and tutors are motivated to continue.

2. How can learners and tutors translate general long-range plans into specific short-term goals?

If learners say they just want "to be able to read and write everything," or make long-range plans such as "get my GED," the tutor can ask questions to help learners narrow their choices to short-term goals by asking:

- What made you decide to come to tutoring just now?
- What do you most want to learn to read and write?
- What numeracy-related things do you want to work on?

- What would you like to do that you can't do now?
- How do you use numbers outside of tutoring sessions?
- What are you reading or writing outside of tutoring sessions?

B. Using the Goals Checklist

1. What is on the list?

The Goals Checklist, on the next page, helps learners identify ways they would like to use, or already use, reading, writing, English, and numbers in their lives. It contains many short-term reading, writing, and numeracy tasks and a number of long-range plans. These goals are grouped into categories of home and family, community, personal interests, consumer issues, communication and technology, work and financial, transportation, education, and English as a second language. Tutors and learners can read the list together and check off one of the columns for each item:

- Filling out the column marked "I Can Do This" is a satisfying reminder of the student's strengths.
- The column "I Want to Work on This" can be used for planning the sessions. Learners who name a large number of items here will also need to decide what to do first.
- The column "I Am Not Interested in This" is a reminder that the learner is the one who decides what to work on or not to work on.
- Later, when the learner is moving toward the goals, accomplishments should be recorded under "I Am Making Progress on This." New goals may then be chosen to replace earlier ones.

Tutors and learners will find it helpful to keep a record of the students' goals to use as a basis for the lessons. It is important to keep track of which goals are accomplished so that students will have the satisfaction of knowing the progress they are making. Literacy agencies, too, can measure their success by the accomplishment of learner goals. For example, The Center for Literacy uses learners' progress toward their goals as one of the measures of success in fulfilling its mission.

Goals Checklist

I Can Do This	I Want to Work on This	I Am Making Progress on This	I Am Not Interested in This	LITERACY TASKS
				Home and Family
				1. Read to children
				2. Help children with homework
				3. Read or write notes to or from child's school
				4. Read or write names of family members or friends
				5. Read or write your own address
				6. Read, write or change recipes
				Community
				7. Participate in religious services
				8. Take part in community activities: block committees
				9. Register to vote
				10. Get a library card
				Personal Interests
				11. Read magazines: Which ones?
				12. Read books: What kind?
				13. Read or write poetry or songs
				14. Keep a journal
				15. Write a family history
				16. Plan a vacation: costs, distance, and time
				Consumer Issues
				17. Read labels
				18. Write shopping lists, read receipts, and figure out change
				19. Estimate and plan for grocery costs
				20. Read menus, or figure out bill, or tip
				21. Improve understanding and planning for utility bills

Goals Checklist

I Can Do This	I Want to Work on This	I Am Making Progress on This	I Am Not Interested in This	LITERACY TASKS
				Communications/Technology
				22. Use the phone book
				23. Read or write letters, notes or cards
				24. Read the newspaper
				25. Communicate by e-mail
				26. Use the Internet to shop
				27. Use the Internet to research community events, directions, and jobs
				Work/Financial
				28. Develop and follow a personal budget
				29. Reading, writing, or math to study for a job
				30. Fill out job applications or other forms
				31. Read help wanted ads
				32. Take a test for a job
				33. Balance a checkbook
				34. Read employee policy/ benefits manual
				35. Read and check math on paycheck
				36. Improve reading or math to get a better job
				37. Read or write occupational vocabulary
				38. Write inventory lists with quantities and costs
				39. Write work reports or time logs
				40. File taxes
				41. Understand/complete forms related to public benefits
				42. Work for yourself, manage your own business

Goals Checklist

I Can Do This	I Want to Work on This	I Am Making Progress on This	I Am Not Interested in This	LITERACY TASKS
				Transportation
				43. Read driver's manual to get license
				44. Read maps or figure distances
				45. Read bus/train schedules
				Education
				46. Get GED or high school diploma
				47. Go to college or technical school
				48. Take a test to advance in your job
				ESL Goals (Non-Native Speakers Only)
				49. Speak to a doctor and describe symptoms
				50. Speak on the telephone
				51. Speak in stores and other public places
				52. Speak with children's teachers
				Other
				53.
				54.
				55.

2. What if everything the student wants seems too hard?

Tutors should not worry if the literacy activities that the learner is interested in seem too difficult. A learner's background knowledge and interests can be of use in working on goals that may appear to require higher literacy skills than the learner seems to have:

- If a poem about a mother-daughter relationship is meaningful to a student, she can read along with the tutor and understand the content, regardless of her ability to read it independently.
- The words in a mechanic's manual may seem to be too difficult for a garage worker who seems able to read very little, but he may be able to read them because he uses them everyday.
- A learner with a strong desire to read the Bible may have many of the passages committed to memory, a useful tool for decoding the written text.

Chapter 3 describes ways to make reading difficult material easier.

3. Choosing new goals

It is important to acknowledge the goals that have been met and set new ones. Learners can master one literacy task but still want instruction in others. For example:

- A student who wanted to read well enough to complete Medicare forms by the time she was sixty-five later began reading to her four-year-old grandson.
- A learner who started because she wanted to read her bills later set the long-range goal of getting a General Educational Development (GED) certificate because she wanted to go to college to be a medical laboratory technician.

The process of recording progress toward goals and setting new ones is a good way to assess learners' accomplishments.

C. Employment Goals

1. Finding a job

Some learners want to find a job as soon as possible. Tutors can show learners how to fill out job applications and how to write resumes. Although finding a job for a student is not a tutor's responsibility, tutors can help learners read want ads or job postings. After one tutor and

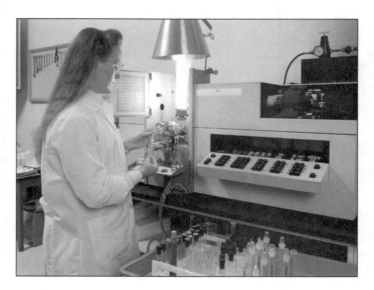

learner pair completed sample job applications, the tutor wrote down the most frequently requested information for the learner to copy and keep in his wallet to refer to during his job search.

2. Getting a promotion

Some learners cannot achieve promotions because the next step up involves writing reports or keeping records. Tutors can help such learners by working on specific job-related reading and writing tasks. One tutor helped his learner write a list of food items she had to order at work. She referred to this list to correctly spell the orders she wrote each week.

3. Job training

Learners who need work may want to consider job training before applying for a job. Tutors and learners should know the following things about employment training:

- Most job training programs require a fairly high level of reading and math and a commitment of a specific amount of time.
- Some job training programs are free of charge to learners on public assistance, and financial aid may be available for those who qualify.
- Loans are often available, but learners should beware of programs which encourage taking out loans but demand repayment even if the training turns out to be inappropriate.

D. Further Educational Goals

If learners were working in an individual or small-group setting, where they achieved success and self-confidence with their tutors, they may decide to change to a class. Learners who do well in lower level classes or programs may choose to move to higher level ones. Adult education from basic literacy to high school equivalency falls into the following categories:

1. Basic Literacy/Adult Basic Education (ABE)

ABE learners are at a low/low-intermediate level. Most do not have a high school diploma. Their ability ranges from knowing only a few words by sight to being able to read short articles on familiar topics. ABE group instruction is offered through non-profit adult education programs, school districts, community colleges, and libraries, but some ABE level learners prefer to work with tutors.

2. Pre-GED and General Educational Development (GED)

GED learners did not finish high school, and want the GED, the high school equivalency degree. GED learners have some proficiency in the five subjects included in the GED test, but they need to brush up on skills before attempting the test. Pre-GED learners have more skills than ABE learners and a desire to attain their GED, but they require more skill development than GED students. The components of the GED test, revised in 2002, are listed on the next page.

3. Adult Diploma

Adult Diploma learners did not finish high school, wish to attain a diploma, and are seeking an option other than the GED. A concept which is growing in popularity, Adult Diploma Programs work with school districts in helping adult learners achieve

actual high school diplomas. Many of these programs, including the one in place at the Center for Literacy, place a high degree of emphasis on independent learning in addition to academic criteria. Learners use their existing life experience while gaining new knowledge toward this diploma.

4. Ongoing improvement

Some learners read and write fairly well and have high school diplomas but feel the need for ongoing improvement in reading, writing, English or numeracy for personal satisfaction, college, or a better job. They may have difficulty reading complex materials such as manuals for their job or in helping their children with tasks involving writing or math. These students may work with tutors or in a class.

THE GED (General Educational Development) Tests

Test	Content Areas		Items	Time Limit
Language Arts, Writing, Part I	Organization	15%	50 Questions	75 minutes
	Sentence Structure	30%		
	Usage	30%		
	Mechanics	25%		
Language Arts, Writing, Part II	Essay		Write an essay on an assigned topic	45 minutes
Social Studies	US History	25%	50 Questions	70 minutes
	World History	15%		
	Civics and Government	25%		
	Economics	20%		
	Geography	15%		
Science	Physical Science	35%	50 Questions	80 minutes
	Life Science	45%		
	Earth/Space Science	20%		
Language Arts, Reading	Nonfiction Texts	25%	40 Questions	65 minutes
	Literary Texts	75%		
Mathematics	Numbers and Operations	20%-30%	Part I: 25 questions with optional use of a calculator	90 minutes
	Measurement and Geometry	20%-30%		
	Data Analysis, Statistics & Probability	20%-30%	Part II: 25 questions without a calculator	
	Algebra, Functions & Patterns	20% -30%		

IV. LEARNING BY DOING

Why is learning by doing effective? We know from experience that any learning project, whether driving a car, running a computer, cooking, or drawing, is most successful when we actually do the activity while learning. Talking, reading, and watching help us understand what we need to do, but we need to do the activity to fully understand and remember it. The learner usually begins by doing small pieces of the task with help, gradually taking on more and more of the task until he is able to do it alone.

Reading and writing: For reading and writing, learners do best when they do real writing and reading for their own purposes, rather than practicing written language through isolated exercises in workbooks. For example:

- If a learner has a goal of attaining a driver's license, she should read the driver's manual. For other goals, learners could use occupational manuals, personal and business mail, recipe books, or computer guides.

- It helps to work in the appropriate setting, if practical, such as a kitchen or computer lab.
- Tutors and learners can take a walk down the street and read everything in sight: street signs; writing on trucks, cars, and buses, as well as license plates and bumper stickers. New items can be copied down by the tutor or learner for study later.
- Tutors and learners may take field trips to libraries, clinics, museums, grocery stores, restaurants, public transportation centers, and various agency offices.

Numeracy: Learners can likewise perform number-related tasks for their own purposes. A learner who wishes to shop economically for groceries can work from grocery store advertisements in the newspaper. Together, tutors and learners can work on a variety of math concepts while meeting the learner's goals.

V. DAILY USE OF READING, WRITING, AND NUMBERS

Why is daily practice necessary? Since learning anything takes not only doing, but repeated practice, and since tutoring sessions are for only a few hours a week, adult literacy learners need to find time to put their learning to use. If tutors and learners look at their own learning experiences, they will realize how much faster they can learn and how much longer they can remember when they get plenty of practice and how quickly they forget if they don't use the newly learned skill right away. Becoming good at baseball, the piano, or using any tool from chain saws to computers all take many hours of experience and practice.

Overcoming obstacles: For adults with responsibilities toward their families, jobs, and communities, finding time outside the tutoring sessions may seem impossible. Learners sometimes are reluctant to attend to their own needs in the face of the demands of a family and a job. A tutor's encouragement might help a learner insist on some time, and maybe a space, to work for herself. Then, tutors and learners can talk about how to make the most of their daily routines.

Everyday tasks: Here are some ways learners can find time to practice:

- Reading signs, pamphlets, as well as magazines or books can take place while traveling on public transportation or while waiting in offices.
- At home, reading labels on containers, captions on television, television guides, and magazines.
- Making lists of things to do each day provides writing experience, followed by the experience of reading the lists at the end of the day to see how many things got done.
- Writing telephone messages, notes to family members, letters, or e-mail all meet everyday needs while providing practice.
- Shopping, paying bills, and planning trips or parties involve working with numbers.

Planning time and location: Tutors and learners can each talk about how they work best, thinking back over their own learning in other areas. Some of us are "morning people," others are "night owls," and we tend to plan our work accordingly. Setting aside time for study takes planning:

- Study is more likely to get done if the learner decides on a specific time each day.
- Even if this study time is as short as half an hour, daily sessions would add up to three and a half hours per week.
- This should be a time of day when the learner has plenty of energy.
- It is important to find a quiet, comfortable place, free from disturbance or distraction.

VI. LOOKING AHEAD

The next chapters discuss adult learning in more detail. They present strategies and materials for helping adult learners in the various aspects of literacy: first reading, then writing, followed by numeracy, and computer use. All these will be related to the principles of collaborative, goal-related, adult learning.

The Whole Reading Experience – Comprehension and Fluency

There are many ways to learn and teach reading, and different people learn in different ways. Tutors and learners should feel free to try as many of the techniques presented here as they see fit and continue to use the ones that work best for them.

This chapter, the first part of a two-chapter focus on reading, presents a variety of strategies for tutors and learners to choose from. The first chapter will focus on reading as a whole activity, in particular, reading fluently and with understanding. The second will focus on parts of the experience: knowing word meanings and being able to identify words on the page.

After a discussion of reading and the needs of adult literacy learners, we present information about reading materials and how to make any reading materials easy to read. Then we discuss how learners are helped by talking about reading, and offer some self-questioning strategies for comprehension and remembering.

I. ABOUT LEARNING TO READ

A. The Balanced Literacy Approach

Learners and tutors may come to tutoring sessions with memories of learning to read in school which are quite different from the literacy teaching which has been found to work best with adults. They may think of working on reading as mainly reading aloud by the students, in the early years especially, with attention to word accuracy and practice exercises focusing on sounds of letters and recognizing words. In the older grades, they may remember reading being taught through short passages, followed by multiple choice questions.

In reality, reading is a complex activity involving much more than saying the right words or getting the one right answer to a question. CFL has found that the most successful reading instruction balances attention among these four elements of reading:

- Comprehension: constructing meaning from text; what reading is all about.
- Fluency: reading text smoothly and rapidly.
- Vocabulary: understanding the meanings of individual words.
- Alphabetics: skills relating to phonemic awareness and decoding.

Comprehension is the goal of all reading, whether you are looking at a STOP sign or a newspaper. The other three elements make comprehension possible. Reading fluently allows the reader to focus on the meaning without consciously paying attention to the individual words. Being able to recognize most of the words and knowing their meanings, as well as knowing how to figure them out by letters or other parts if they're unfamiliar, is also necessary for comprehension, although it does not guarantee it.

These elements can be combined by starting out doing the whole reading experience of reading for comprehension, followed by working on its parts as needed. A session can begin with the learner reading, for comprehension and fluency, something related to his goals, followed by doing some learning activities to improve any of the reading elements: comprehension, fluency, vocabulary, or word identification, and closing by doing the whole reading experience again, perhaps silently.

B. How Do People Improve at Reading?

Literacy learners need four things:

1. Material that is important and relevant to them. If people value what they read:
   - They will comprehend better, using what they already know about the subject to help them think as they read.
   - They will read more, so that their improvement will start a helpful cycle of reading more, improving, and finding more things they are able and eager to read.

2. Reading with someone who can make the task easier. The tutor's role is to serve as a scaffold, providing support as the learner takes the next step toward independence. One of the tutor's roles is to use strategies, which will be described later, to bring goal-related material within the learner's reach.

3. Receiving feedback. Another of the tutor's roles is to help the learner do the task the right way.

4. Experience actually reading. The more time people spend doing anything they want to improve in, the faster they will progress.

II. WORKING TOGETHER ON READING

A. What to Read?

Learners' own dictated stories: To get new learners reading right away, no matter what their ability, tutors can help them read the stories the tutor writes down as they tell them.

Use the Goals Checklist: Materials for adult learners cover a wide range to meet a variety of student goals or purposes. Many of the literacy materials learners might want or need will be found in or suggested by the Goals Checklist, described in Chapter 2.

Use slightly challenging materials: Since people learn best when they are somewhat challenged, but not frustrated, they can read aloud, or on their own, materials for which the learner needs help with approximately one in every 10 or 20 words.

Use special strategies for harder material: Materials that the learner really wants but are frustrating, requiring help with about one out of every five words, can be read by using the strategies for making reading easier described in Section B, Making Challenging Material Easier.

1. Material from everyday life

One of the most useful types of reading material for adult literacy students is the printed matter from everyday life. Most learners have been experiencing literacy challenges every day and felt anxiety when they could not read what they needed to read. Even if they have developed ways to get around or hide their difficulties, they will be relieved to start working on these daily challenges.

The materials that would actually be used in that situation are the best to use. Learners can be encouraged to begin reading more of the printed material around them and to bring in whatever they wanted. For example, the learners can bring in:

- pamphlets
- mail advertisements and catalogs
- food or other product boxes, labels, or instructions
- information from their job

- notices or homework from children's schools
- political information
- public transportation schedules
- menus from take-out restaurants
- church programs

The tutor or agency staff might supply:

- driver's manuals
- vocational or technical booklets
- maps
- travel brochures
- crossword puzzles

2. Fiction and non-fiction

Stories, plays, poems and articles provide entertainment and knowledge to learners who want to read for pleasure, to learn more about the world around them, or for personal enrichment or for professional development. Many literacy organizations help their tutors and learners get started with books chosen to match the interests expressed by the student at the initial interview.

Since the interests and needs of the learner dictate what materials to use, tutors and learners can discuss what to read and how to find it. They can ask for new materials from literacy organization staff or bring in books, magazines or newspapers from home, the library, or elsewhere. With Internet access at their library or literacy organization, they can find information on any topic, including current or back issues of newspapers.

a) How can we find easy reading meant for adults?

Many libraries and literacy organizations order books specially written for adult new readers. There are many publishers who print books of adult new reader interest. One of the most popular is New Readers Press. The American Library Association (www.ala.org/PLA) publishes an annual list of top titles for adult new readers.

Books in this category include a wide range of subjects and a variety of levels of difficulty. Many of them are short pieces of realistic fiction on subjects of interest to adults, written in a style that is comfortable for new readers. They describe ordinary people dealing with such situations as a new job or a divorce. There are books about mystery, romance, adventure, family life, and religion, as well as self-help books on such topics as child care, or auto maintenance. These books are usually illustrated, and the words and sentences are fairly short so that adult new readers are often pleased to find themselves finishing a book for the first time in their lives.

b) What does the newspaper offer?

The newspaper covers a wide range of possible student interests. Besides providing a wealth of news information, it helps with consumer needs, vocational and educational opportunities, as well as announcements of community events.

Which parts are read, and how, depends on the learner's interests and ability. Here are some suggestions:

- Look at the full-page grocery store advertisements for words to make a shopping list.
- Read photo captions, headlines, and score charts of athletic events.
- Read the advice columns, and write or dictate answers to the letters.
- Read the comics together, taking parts, as in a play.
- Learn to find your way around a want ad section.

The web site http://www.press-enterprise.com/nie helps learners to use newspapers. The site is written with elementary and high school teachers in mind, but tutors can turn the "teacherish" tone of the assignments into the shared decision-making by talking with learners. Some helpful suggestions under "Tips" include: "Just read it: Set aside time to read the newspaper each day for no other reason than enjoyment to help develop the reading habit." The "Ideas" menu includes sections on "Life Skills" and "Critical Thinking," and "Teaching Help" provides links to current and back issues for newspapers all over the U.S. and to editorial cartoons from all over the world.

Even if the main text of news stories is too difficult for literacy learners, no part of the newspaper is beyond any student's reach because the tutor can read with the learner, using the strategies described in the section, "Making Challenging Material Easier."

c) Should tutors and students use children's books?

We do not recommend using books written for children to teach adults, because it is belittling to adult learners to suggest that they have the same interests as children. On the other hand, children's books are perfect for any adult learner who wants to read to children. Good children's books, many with beautiful artwork, can capture the hearts of young and old. Many of the "chapter books" written for young adults, both fiction and non-fiction, can be appreciated by an adult learner. Some of the advantages are:

- They are fun to hear.
- The illustrations are appealing.
- The illustrations make them easier to understand.
- Picture books, or a chapter of a longer book, can be read in a single session, making them less intimidating.
- They can be reread with pleasure.
- Adults can read them at deeper levels than children, as they bring to them their own life experience.
- The books are readily available in public libraries.

These guiding questions from Betty Ansin Smallwood of the Center for Adult English Language Acquisition may help learners and tutors to find an appropriate book:

- Does it include adult characters?
- Does it cover mature themes or carry universal messages?
- Do the illustrations help tell the story?
- Does it contain repeated, predictable language patterns that make it easier to read?
- Does its language seem close to the learner's ability to understand?

d) What can we find on the Internet?

Tutors and learners who have Internet access can find a wealth of material on this powerful tool, including suggestions for tutoring plans, new trends and ideas for tutoring, as well as reading materials. Using search engines such as Google, learners can find many articles of interest, and they can access entire books online, reading whenever they can get to a computer. There is more information on the uses of computers in Chapter 6 of this manual as well as in the Bibliography.

e) Why use learner-written materials?

Learners at any level are usually very interested in reading what other learners have written. Such materials are useful for the following reasons:

- They are interesting because they come out of experiences that the learners can relate to.

- They are easy to read because they are written in familiar vocabulary and speech patterns.

- They motivate the learners who read them to write their own pieces.

Where can we find learner-written materials? Many literacy agencies publish materials written by their own learners, and most can supply information on similar materials from elsewhere. For example, every year the Center for Literacy publishes a booklet of student writing, from which learners read their work to family and friends at the annual "Speak Out" event.

3. Learner-dictated materials: The language experience approach

Reading what they have dictated for their tutors to write down helps learners who can read very little on their own. It is a good activity for the first session. It breaks the ice and provides material for future sessions.

a) Why should new readers read their own dictated stories?

Their own stories are effective teaching tools for these reasons:

- They will be easier than other materials because they are in the vocabulary and speech patterns that the learners have used all of their lives.

- They will be easier to understand and relate to because they record the learners' own ideas and experiences.

- Seeing their own words in print helps link oral language and written language. Learners can say, "So that's what that word looks like!"

- The activity gets new literacy learners started on the first step of writing.

This approach can also be helpful for more advanced learners. It helps learners who have a lot to say spell words that they may want to use but have difficulty spelling, and it helps learners who face particularly challenging writing tasks, such as writing letters for a job search, create a first draft.

b) How can learners create their own reading materials?

In the Language Experience Approach, the learner dictates a story to the tutor or someone else, who takes down the learner's exact words.

This is the procedure:

- The tutor explains that she will be the learner's secretary, writing down just what the student says, and after the story is on paper, they can read it together.

- The tutor asks, "What would you like to tell about?" If this question is not enough to start an experience story, the learner could suggest choosing from these topics:

  Home or school memories.

  Portraits of family members or friends.

  An opinion about a current issue.

  A list of goals, or of things to remember to do.

- Getting the story on paper: The tutor should write down what the learner says, word for word, without changing the learner's speech patterns. This is not an exercise in the conventions of Standard English. Any changes can be made later if the learner wants them.

  The tutor prints, as neatly as possible, on every other line.

  The tutor can ask the learner to slow down, if necessary.

- Making copies: A copy should be made for reading at future sessions and for the learner to reread at home.

- When to stop: Learners will probably be ready to stop after a few sentences. The learner can think up a title, and the date and learner's name should be included.

c) What can we do once the story is written?

The learner's own story is a perfect source for any reading activity. Here are some suggestions:

- For the first reading, the tutor can read the story as the learner listens and looks at the text.

- For repeated readings, the story can be read using any of the ways of reading together described in Section B.

- After a few readings, words of one copy can be cut out and rearranged, either to put the original sentences together again or to make new ones.

- The learner could copy the story as an introductory writing activity.

B. Making Challenging Material Easier

How does reading with the tutor help learners? As we have said, people learn by doing, with help, what they can almost do alone. With the tutor as model, reading together allows learners to practice reading fluently, focusing on the meaning without stopping to struggle for individual words. The tutor's voice can help with comprehension by supplying words the learner does not recognize. Repetition is helpful, moving from more supported to less supported methods.

Five strategies for reading together are listed below, starting with listening, which is the most supported one, and ending with silent reading, which is the most independent. These strategies can be used with any interesting material and with any level student, matching the method with the amount of help needed.

Learners and tutors often expect to spend most of their tutoring time with the learner reading aloud to the tutor. However, this is often the most threatening method for them because it makes reading feel like a performance, rather than the meaning-making activity that it should be. Many students have unhappy memories of being laughed at in school for making mistakes and need to use the more supported ways of reading before being asked to read aloud.

1. Listening while looking

The learner listens to the tutor or another learner read, while looking at the page.

a) How is this helpful?

Listening is useful for material which learners could not read alone, needing help with one out of about ten words. It allows learners to start working toward their goals regardless of what they can read on their own. It is also useful for more advanced learners when they want to read material that is extremely difficult for them. Comprehension takes place through listening, while the learners learn the words by seeing them.

b) How is it done?

The learner can listen to the tutor, to a more advanced student, or to a tape recording of a book.

- The learner can listen the first time without looking at the page, if it helps to get the idea; but on the second reading, the learner should follow along, matching the reader's voice with the words on the page.

- The person reading aloud should read at a normal pace.
- Pausing briefly at the end of each sentence allows the person reading aloud to keep the reader from going too fast.
- The learner and tutor can decide how much to read at a time, and how much rereading to do.

c) Getting practice: Listening to a tape at home

As we have said, learners of any skill will progress faster with lots of practice. Listening to tapes at home is an excellent way for a new reader learner to read books that she could not handle without help.

Many books for new readers come with tapes. If tapes are not already available, these books are so short that it is not hard for a tutor with a tape recorder to make her own. A tutor, a more advanced student, or another volunteer, could help by making the tape. To get an idea of the story, the learner could listen while the tutor plays all or part of the tape during the session.

The learner can practice listening to a tape during the tutoring session, to get used to the equipment and the procedure. A person who is listening to tapes for the first time can do this:

- Listen to a short section, one or two minutes, without looking at the book.
- Start the tape again, opening the book, and listening to the same section of the tape while following in the book, playing and rereading the section as often as needed.
- After several readings, try reading the section without listening, going back to the tape if necessary.

2. Echo reading

In this strategy, the learner alternates between listening and speaking, echoing the tutor who reads a phrase or a sentence at a time. While listening, the learner reads along on the page, then looks back and repeats what she heard, matching it with the words she sees on the page.

a) How does it help?

This approach is helpful for basic level learners who recognize very few words and need help with the stories written for new readers. The learner comprehends by listening and learns to recognize words by matching what she hears with what she sees.

b) How is it done?

While looking at the print, the learner echoes a phrase or a sentence at a time after the tutor, or another more advanced reader, says it. The learner hears and remembers what was said, matching it with the words on the page. A little practice together will show the leader how long to read before stopping.

To be most effective:

- The pieces of text read need to be long enough to have meaning.
- They should be short enough for the learner to be able to remember.

c) What can learners use?

Poems are good for this method, as you can stop after each line, and rhyme, rhythm, and repetition often make reading easier by setting a pattern. This method works well with materials which the learner can read with help, needing help with about one word in ten.

3. Duet reading

As in a piano duet, the learner reads aloud at the same time as another person, perhaps lagging a word or two behind as people do when singing an unfamiliar song in a group. Duet reading is harder to do than echo reading because learners do not hear the words read in advance.

a) How does this help?

This way of reading can help to speed up learners who have gotten in the habit of reading so slowly, word by word, that they don't think about how the words work together to express the meaning.

b) What does the tutor need to do?

The tutor needs to find materials that the learner can read fairly easily. A learner-dictated story would be an excellent choice, as would anything with familiar and colorful language, such as poems, speeches, or Bible passages.

The tutor should:

- Read at a normal pace.
- Run a finger under the words being read.
- Reduce pressure on the learner by explaining that the goal here is smooth reading rather than comprehension.
- As the learner gains in proficiency, the tutor can begin to read more softly, letting the learner's voice take over.

4. Guided oral reading

The learner reads aloud, with the tutor assisting as needed. Once learners become familiar with the material, they usually enjoy reading aloud by themselves, but as we have said, it can be one of the most uncomfortable ways of reading. It may bring up painful memories of classroom experiences of struggling for unknown words in front of the whole class. Learners usually do best by using more supported ways first.

a) Making it easier by taking turns.

One way of making the learner feel less pressured is to do it with the tutor and learner each taking turns reading sections of the material, so the tutor can model reading with the expression that reflects the meaning.

- The tutor begins reading while the learner tracks silently for several words.
- The tutor stops, and the learner reads the next several words, stopping for the tutor to begin again.
- In larger tutor/learner groupings, small groups and pairs can read aloud, taking turns on a volunteer basis, and beginning and ending when they feel ready to.
- As learners gain confidence, they will start increasing the length of their turns.

b) How can the tutor help with hard words?

Since guided oral reading is intended to improve comprehension and fluency, it should not be interrupted too often for figuring out words. Here are some tips on helping:

- The tutor should not interrupt to correct oral reading errors that do not affect the meaning.
- If a mistake does change the meaning, the tutor could ask the learner to look at the mistaken word again.
- If a learner hesitates over a word, someone else may help out.

   The tutor can ask the learner if he or she wants the help.

   The tutor should supply the word if it seems that struggling with it would either be unsuccessful or take so long that it would distract from the meaning of the whole.

- When a learner does want help, the tutor can do the following:

    If the context would help, ask, "What would make sense here?"

    If the word is phonetically spelled, ask, "Can you sound out the letters?"

    If the word is complicated, and pronunciation isn't important, just recognition, as in a last name or a scientific term, the learner could be urged to just remember what it looks like and what it refers to.

    If looking forward or back to find the word elsewhere would help, the tutor could suggest one or the other.

- Words missed during the reading may be listed for use later in some of the instructional activities as described in the next chapter.

c) Which materials work best with oral reading?

Stories, plays, and poems, are particularly enjoyable when read aloud, as long as the readers are comfortable with the material.

5. Silent reading

a) Why is silent reading valuable for all levels of learners?

Experienced readers prefer to read silently because it is faster, with the message going straight from the eye to the brain. Silent reading is also valuable for those with a limited reading vocabulary who cannot read many materials without help.

- It provides practice conveniently: One of the advantages of silent reading is that it can be done where other people are around. Since learners need all the practice they can get, they should be encouraged to try reading silently on the bus, in a doctor's waiting room, or anywhere else that they have time to fill.

- It provides practice in comprehension checking: When they are reading silently on their own, learners have a chance to practice checking their own comprehension. When the tutor is not there to provide help with individual words, the learner has to be the one who decides whether the material makes sense, and to go back and reread and figure out what was missed. How to teach self-questioning for comprehension will be discussed later in this chapter.

b) Why should we read silently during the tutoring session?

It is helpful for getting people used to reading on their own, and it helps them to trust their own judgment in deciding what to read.

c) How can we do it?

- Tutors and learners can set aside a few minutes, perhaps at the end of the session, each reading independently their own books or other materials.

- After they have been reading a few minutes, they should talk a bit, giving each other some idea of what they read and their thoughts about it.

- The tutor does not have to worry about word-perfect reading here, as the goal is general comprehension. As long as the learner feels the material made sense and is able to talk about it, the reading was successful.

d) What is the best kind of material to read silently?

It should be interesting. Even if it is fairly hard for the learner, he can still flip through it, looking at any pictures, captions, or short pieces such as advertisements, quizzes, letters or cartoons.

If learners don't understand enough to stay interested, they should try again with one of the more supported methods such as echo reading.

6. Matching the technique, the material, and the learner

There may initially be some trial and error in choosing the most effective reading technique. Predicting difficulty is hard because so many factors can make a piece easy or hard for a given student.

How can we tell whether something will be easy or hard? The surest way is to let the learner try it for a few pages. Does it hold his interest? Does he have trouble with more than one word in every ten?

Labels as to "reading level" are often misleading. Some books for adult new readers are labeled by levels corresponding to elementary school grades. Formulas for these were developed about fifty years ago based on word and sentence length, but since then educators have realized that the reader's relation to the material, why it is being read, how it is written, and how it looks on the page affect difficulty, too. Learners find reading material easier if it is:

- interesting or familiar.
- fairly short.
- about people, rather than information or ideas.
- written with a small number of ideas per sentence and per paragraph.
- printed large, with plenty of white space and illustrations.

The following list summarizes which techniques are most helpful at different difficulty levels:

a) If the material is challenging, with the learner needing help with more than one in every five of the words, or if it is being read for information, such as a driver's manual, the learner can use, in the following order:

- Listening
- Echo reading

b) If the material is fairly easy, with the learner needing help with more or less one in every ten words, and is being read for entertainment, the best methods might be:

- Duet reading
- Guided oral reading

c) If the material is easy for the learner, and is being read for entertainment, such as a story, a play, or a joke, the student may choose between:

- Guided oral reading
- Silent reading

All these ways of reading together help the learner to read fluently, without stopping at every potential problem. This aids comprehension by allowing the learner to focus on the meaning of the entire piece rather than individual words.

C. A Strategy for Comprehension: Filling in Blanks

A comprehension exercise known as the cloze technique, where learners supply missing words, is useful to redirect the attention of those who focus so hard on the parts of reading, getting each word right, that they miss the meaning of the whole. This technique is discussed again in the next chapter because it can also be used to help learners figure out words whose meaning they don't know.

1. What is a cloze exercise?

It is a short passage with missing words which the reader fills in. It is made like this:
- Approximately every fifth word has been removed.
- The learner reads the passage aloud, supplying the missing words by thinking about the meaning that is suggested by the surrounding words.

2. How does the cloze technique help learners?

The blanks represent words that the learner cannot read. By reading a passage with words removed, the learner creates meaning out of the remaining words. These are the benefits:

- The learner gets a more accurate idea of reading as an active process of making meaning rather than reciting words.
- The learner gains in confidence when he realizes he can comprehend a passage even if he doesn't recognize or understand every word.

3. How is a cloze exercise made?

- Use short sections from magazine or newspaper articles, or the student's own writing.
- With white correction fluid or a computer, remove approximately every fifth word. To make the exercise easier:

  Remove the small, connecting words, such as "to" and "from," because they are the easiest to predict.

  Remove words whose meanings are suggested by other words.

  Leave the words which are crucial to the meaning and could not be figured out.

The following cloze exercise, made from a student's own story, has approximately every fifth word removed but essential words left in:

To Be Able to See is Wonderful

Riding on the subway I _____ the opportunity to meet _____ people of all ages _____ with many personalities. It _____ me a lot of _____ reasons to reach out _____ say "hello" to someone _____ is sitting near and _____ need a helping hand. _____ my traveling I came _____ a young blind lady _____ touched my heart. At _____ same time she built _____ up to the point _____ she made me _____ blessed because she was _____ home from work.

This young _____ was so happy about _____ life. She couldn't even _____, but she was working _____ computers for a living. _____ I sat feeling bad _____ sad for no reason. She _____ very up-building for _____. I just wanted to _____ about it because it _____ in my mind. When _____ can see, be happy _____ work harder at _____ constructive, and give thanks _____ all you are.

By Carrie Nesmith

4. How does the learner do it? It is done this way:

- The tutor encourages the learner to read the passage and supply the missing words by asking, "What would make sense here?"

- The learner fills in the blanks orally.

- The tutor reminds the learner that there is no single right answer; anything that makes sense is acceptable.

D. Talking Together for Comprehension

1. Talking before, during and after reading

Reading comprehension – the making of meaning – takes place before, during, and after the reading of a text. During these three phases, the successful reader predicts what the materials will be about before reading, monitors his understanding while reading, and reacts personally to what is read afterwards.

a) Why is talking about the reading the best way to work on comprehension?

It is a natural and pleasant activity. Many people talk to their friends and co-workers about their reading as they share books, greeting cards, and other printed information. It is helpful for tutors and learners to discuss the learner's understanding, questions, and opinions about the reading. Comprehension is enriched when several readers share their responses to a reading, including talking about any of their experiences which the reading reminds them of.

Tutors can help adult learners focus on meaning by talking about everything that is read – before, during, and after reading. As good readers read, they are constantly imagining what will come next and relating the text to their own knowledge and opinions. This kind of talk prepares the learner for the kind of thinking that good readers do while reading.

b) How can tutors help learners do what good readers do?

Before reading – what good readers do: Good readers begin the process of comprehension before they look at the page. For example, as a person reaches for a newspaper, a question based on yesterday's news may come to mind. A glance at the headlines tells what the article will be about. The reader starts predicting the information in that article and brings to mind what he already knows about the topic.

Tutors can help learners prepare for comprehension in several ways. After helping the learner to select a topic, set a purpose for reading and find material, they can ask the learner to do the following:

- Confirm the purpose: Why did they choose this selection?

- Relate the text to their own experience by looking at the pictures, title, and chapter headings.

- Predict what will be in the selection based on the pictures, title, and chapter headings.

- Raise questions that they hope the text will answer, especially if they are reading for information.

During reading – what good readers do: While reading the story, a good reader gets new information which may confirm or contradict what she already knew or which may add to her knowledge of the subject. As she goes along, she decides whether she is getting what she wants out of the story, and whether to continue or stop reading. Most important of all, she checks her comprehension, rereading sections that seem unclear, and making notes if necessary.

The tutor can urge the learner to ask herself some of the following questions to help monitor and help with comprehension:

- Is this making sense to me?

- How does this compare with what I expected?

- How does it relate to my own experience?

- What do I think will happen next?

- What do I think of this?

- Do I want to keep reading this?

The tutor should assure the learner that if anything doesn't make sense, the learner can always interrupt the reading to reread problematic sections. If necessary, he can mark the passage as problematic, perhaps noting unfamiliar words the tutor could help with later.

After reading – what good readers do: After a good reader has finished reading, she continues to evaluate the new information. She can review any questions she had before reading, to see if they were answered, and if any new ones have been raised. She can also decide how much of the article she values or believes and how much she dislikes or doubts. She may think about how the story changed her opinions or feelings about people or about life, and may even change her as a person.

The tutor and learners can talk about the selection, discussing open-ended questions which encourage individual thinking rather than just remembering, such as:

- Which of my questions were answered; which weren't?
- What new questions did it raise?
- Does it make sense to me; was it believable?
- Did I enjoy it; do I want to read other stories (articles or poems) like it?
- What did I learn from it?
- What meaning does it have for me?

2. Asking thought-provoking questions

Questions are excellent for making people think, and different kinds of questions call on different levels of comprehension. How the reader wants to understand a text depends on what he is reading and why. The learner's ability has nothing to do with it. A learner at any level might be reading a short story for entertainment, and stay on the simplest level of understanding, or adult learners reading materials written at an easy level may enjoy thinking about these materials at a deeper level. A learner whose goals include going to college will need to be able to analyze reading materials in complex ways.

We can think of comprehension as falling into three types or levels, listed here from least to most sophisticated. Tutors can help learners move from one level of comprehension to the next by asking different types of questions.

a) Literal comprehension

Literal comprehension means understanding what was actually stated in the material, "getting the message." It tends to answer questions of fact, usually starting with: who, what, when, or where. This is the level of comprehension that the learner and the tutor may think of first when they consider dealing with comprehension.

While literal comprehension is important, there are problems, at any level of ability, with limiting questions to this level. It leaves out important aspects of reading, denying the adult learner the enriching experiences of reading on higher levels. Focusing on "the facts" alone leads to the pattern of asking questions with only one right answer, to be judged by the person asking the question. The exchange feels more like a test than a conversation between two adults working together for a shared goal. Here are some tips on making the most of literal comprehension:

- Literal comprehension is essential when reading for information, such as a driver's manual.

- One way to check on literal comprehension without making it feel like a test is for the tutor to ask the learner about what he thinks are the most important facts or to give a summary.

- Another indirect way to check for literal comprehension is to ask learners to give specific facts from the text, after they have offered an opinion or read "between the lines." (Ask: "Can you tell me what in the text makes you think that?")

If the learner seems to have missed a great deal of the literal meaning, it would be wise to go back to reread the piece and read using an easier method, such as listening, before working on higher levels of comprehension.

b) Interpretive comprehension

Interpretive comprehension means "reading between the lines," understanding what was implied, rather than what was stated, in the material. It helps the learner to connect what was read to what she read earlier, or what she already knew.

- Rather than using the factual question words listed above, a tutor can assess interpretive comprehension by starting questions with why, what if, and how.

- In reading a story, they could discuss:

  why the characters act as they do

  how the author feels about any character

  how they feel about any character

- In reading for information, the readers could:

  speculate about a newspaper writer's attitude to the topic

  analyze the strategies behind advertisements

Questions inviting interpretation are usually open-ended, with no single right answer, and so are more interesting and enjoyable to discuss than those for literal comprehension. The tutor and learner are in an equal relationship, sharing opinions like members of a reading group.

c) Applied comprehension is the most challenging.

It involves applying what was stated or implied in the text to a different context, based on the learner's own experience or knowledge. Applied comprehension may be thought of as "reading beyond the lines." This is the level of reading comprehension that will often be called upon with higher academic writing, but it is by no means limited to the college-bound.

For example, a reader might apply:

- Ideas learned from a gardening article to parenting strategies.
- A story from Greek mythology to her personal life.

E. Visual Questioning Strategies for Comprehension and Memory

The process of formulating questions, organizing ideas, and writing them down helps with both understanding and remembering. We present two graphic organizers, techniques for organizing information around questions that work well for comprehending and remembering material, whether for academic study or personal growth.

Charts for the two techniques, Survey, Question, Read, Recite, Review (SQ3R) and Know-Want-Learn (K-W-L) are provided in this manual, but they can be created by hand, on the computer, or downloaded from the Internet by typing in either set of the initials and opening items containing the word "generator."

1. SQ3R: Survey – Question – Read – Recite – Review

This five-step approach offers new readers an organized approach to comprehending and learning information, especially in longer pieces that would take more than one session to complete.

Surveying is done by:
- Reading the title.
- Reading the introduction and/or summary.

- Reading each bold-face heading and subheading.
- Reviewing the graphics.
- Reviewing any other reading aids, such as italics, definitions, or asterisks.

Questioning is done by:

- Turning headings or bold-faced materials into one or more questions that might be answered by the passage.
- Writing these questions down.

Reading is done by:

- Reading one section at a time.
- Adding questions, if necessary.
- Focusing on main ideas rather than details.
- Looking for the answers to the reader's questions and writing them down.

Reciting is done after each section, by:

- Covering the answers to the questions written earlier.
- Reciting the answers, then uncovering them.
- Rereading the passage if answers cannot be correctly recalled.

Reviewing is done by:

- Reciting answers to all section questions again, after all sections of the chapter have been read, using the previous techniques.
- Rereading the relevant section to find any answers that cannot be recalled.

2. K-W-L: Know – Want – Learn

K-W-L is a useful tool for a learner who is reading to upgrade his knowledge or skills in a particular area. If a learner is reading the driver's manual to get a a license, for example, he may use this technique to assess what knowledge he already has about driving, predict what he needs to learn from the manual, and after the reading, assess whether what he learned met his needs.

The method uses a three-column chart on which the learners answer these questions:

- What do I already know about the topic?
- What do I want to know about the topic? or What do I think I will learn from the reading?
- What have I learned about the topic?

How to use a K-W-L chart:

1. On a chalkboard or as a handout, learners see the chart (illustrated below).

2. As learners talk, the tutor or the learners write down, in the columns, everything that fits.

3. Before reading, learners identify, and learners or the tutor enter in the "K" column everything that they know about the topic

4. Before reading, for the "W" column, learners tell and record survey headings and graphics to predict what they will learn, or hope to learn, from the reading.

5. After reading, for the "L" column, learners tell and record:

   All that they have learned from the passage, noting any misconceptions that they had in the W column.

   Their feelings about their general understanding of the passage.

K	W	L

A full size chart is available for copying on the following page.

IV. CONCLUSION

In this chapter we have focused on the whole experience of reading, developing proficiency in fluency and comprehension through experience with meaningful text. Now we are ready to look at the parts. Since the reading experience includes interpreting words and letters, the next chapter provides strategies for developing the other two elements of reading: vocabulary, or the meaning of words, and recognition or decoding of words.

K	W	L

Chapter 4

The Parts of Reading: Working With Words

I. OPPORTUNISTIC TEACHING: USING THE "TEACHABLE MOMENT"

For working on the parts of reading, as opposed to the whole experience, Center for Literacy has found opportunistic teaching, working on a topic as the need for it arises, more effective than doing it in a preplanned order. This approach is especially appropriate for adult learners.

Why is opportunistic teaching helpful for adult learners? Adults benefit from opportunistic teaching for several reasons.

- Adults, with their life experience, already know a lot, so complete coverage of a topic may be unnecessary.
- Adults want their learning to be relevant to their needs.

How does opportunistic teaching apply to reading instruction? As we said in the last chapter, people get better at reading by doing a great deal of it. When learners get stuck on particular words while doing guided oral reading, the tutor can teach opportunistically. For example, as described in Chapter 3, the tutor can keep track of words the learner needed help with. He can look for patterns, such as the ending -tion, or words with many syllables, and teach the needed skill, right after the reading is finished. Working this way makes for more effective teaching, and also makes lesson planning, which is discussed in more detail in Chapter 8, easier.

All the knowledge and skills presented in this chapter can be taught opportunistically. This means using learners' experiences, reading goal-related materials, or the whole experience, to reveal which parts of the reading experience can be taught directly.

II. BUILDING VOCABULARY: WORDS AND MEANINGS

Vocabulary study, knowing the meaning of the words, is comprehension narrowed down to the word level. The comprehension activities in the last chapter will help learners read better, but a reader who has trouble with the meaning of too many words in a passage will still have trouble grasping its main idea.

How can tutors help learners add new words to their vocabularies? Tutors can combine broad reading, where learners will be exposed to many words, with direct teaching about using the context and the meaning of the words themselves. These break into four activities:

- Providing exposure to new words in a meaningful situation.
- Teaching and encouraging learners to use the context while reading.
- Directly teaching words and meanings.
- Practicing newly learned words.

A. Repeated Exposure in Context

1. How do we know repeated exposure in context works?

Our own experience shows us that we learned most of the words we know by repeatedly hearing or reading them. We gradually figured out what they meant from the situation, or what else was being said, and we remember the ones we kept hearing and using. In the earliest years of our lives, through childhood, we learned to understand words by hearing them again and again. As adults, we continue to pick up new words the same way. People who read a lot learn many words from seeing them in print. They might not use all these words in ordinary conversation, but the words become part of their reading vocabulary. Adults also find new words when they start a new hobby or job or move to a new place.

2. How can adult literacy learners learn new words from reading them?

A learner reading more challenging material, such as the newspaper, a novel, or technical information, is likely to meet unfamiliar words. Some of the vocabulary growth from reading will happen automatically. Learners will read words that they weren't sure of, getting a clearer idea of their meaning each time they see them in use. Words may be learned unconsciously when the context makes them clear.

3. How can a tutor help learners pick up new words through reading?

a) Increase exposure with varied and daily reading

If a reader is exposed to rich and diverse reading materials, he will be exposed to a wide variety of words. Tutors should encourage their readers to find things to read outside of the tutoring session, as well as during them. Tutors can help by encouraging learners to read to meet a variety of interests and needs, such as: driving, home repair, parenting, health history, and entertainment.

b) Teach learners to learn new words through context

Learners may think direct vocabulary study is the only way to learn new words. While they have been discovering meaning through context all their lives, they may not trust themselves to do so while reading. It is helpful for tutors to remind learners that context use worked for them in the past and guide them in doing so in their current reading. The tutor can ask a question that focuses back on the context, as in this exchange:

- The learner says of the word "famished" in her reading, "I don't know what that word means."

- The tutor suggests, "Let's take a look at the whole sentence. What do you think it might mean?"

- The tutor says the word to give the pronunciation, and either one of them can read the sentence: "By night time she was famished because she hadn't eaten since early morning."

- The learner says, "Oh, hungry," and the tutor says, "Yes, 'starving'! You see how reading the rest of it helped?"

c) Practice context use with the cloze technique

The cloze technique was recommended in the previous chapter as a strategy for improving comprehension. Reading passages with some of the words left blank helps learners practice making sense out of not only the text as a whole, but also of individual words.

To find word meanings: In a cloze exercise for learning vocabulary, a sentence is presented with an empty space in the place of the unknown word. Of course, for this to work, the surrounding words have to provide clues as to the meaning of the unfamiliar word. For example, the tutor could use this sentence, with the word "vindictive," which the student didn't know, removed:

"I'm never going to forgive them. I'm a very _____ person."

The learner fills in this blank with a word such as, "unforgiving." If the learner is a bit off track, saying "jealous," for example, the tutor can refine the definition.

The tutor needs to make sure the learner understands the purpose of the cloze exercise, by stating these points:

- The goal of this exercise is to learn a strategy for figuring out the unfamiliar words in any reading.

- In his reading, the learner can imagine any unknown word as a blank and look for its meaning in the rest of the sentence.

Doing a few cloze exercises this way gives people practice and confidence about making sensible guesses based on the surrounding words.

B. Direct Instruction: Words and Definitions

Direct teaching of vocabulary is needed when the context isn't enough to supply the meaning of a word. Direct instruction is also useful when a learner prefers a systematic, measurable approach to building vocabulary or wants to increase his vocabulary on a certain topic, such as health services. The direct approach to vocabulary learning is focused; learners can quickly zero in on words, learn them, and know what they have accomplished. Lists of words are helpful as reminders of what to work on and review.

Most people remember direct vocabulary instruction from school: memorizing lists of words with definitions and reading and writing them in sample sentences demonstrating their use, with tests on the definitions on Friday. The hope was that when these words were met later in books or conversation, they would be recognized and understood. The risk of this approach is that words and definitions memorized from a list are likely to be forgotten after the test.

1. How can tutors best use direct instruction with adult literacy learners?

a) Provide definitions

The best vocabulary definitions are usually the ones tutors provide. They will probably be easier to understand and remembered better than a dictionary definition. The tutor can explain it in terms of what the learner already knows. The meaning can be fine-tuned with a dictionary later if desired. A good definition might include:

- Another word with the same meaning.
- Another word with a similar meaning and an explanation of the difference between the two.
- A sentence or two explaining the word.
- Examples of the word in use.

b) Use the dictionary

The dictionary comes in handy for words that are hard to explain or unfamiliar to the tutor. Learners who read well enough to find the words and identify the right definition will find it a useful tool. If needed, tutors can teach learners these skills:

- To find the word alphabetically, look beyond its first letter, to the second, then third, and fourth, as far as you need to.

- To find the right definition, if there are more than one, look back at the sentence in which the word was found.

2. How can tutors make remembering easier?

These strategies can counteract the tendency to forget words learned in lists:

a) Study words found by the learner

The act of choosing and copying is a first step in learning.

- Learners at any level should be alert to any unknown words in their reading.

- The tutor should encourage the learner to ask whenever he doesn't know what a word in his reading material means.

- The tutor can supply the word's meaning without interrupting the reading, but should write it down for practicing later if desired.

Tutors and learners can put together a collection of words from various sources:

- Magazines, books and manuals that relate to the learner's goals and interests. Whatever a learner's interests are, there is vocabulary associated with each one:

  - reading the sports section

  - learning to play a musical instrument

- Policy manuals, job descriptions, or want ads can help with:

  - learning more about an occupation

  - finding a job

b) Record the words in a notebook

A vocabulary notebook is a valuable memory aid. A learner who wants to build his vocabulary needs to get in the habit of noticing and writing down unfamiliar words, whether found through reading or listening.

- At home, the learner can copy words from anything he is reading.

- He can try to write down, guessing at spelling, words he hears, in person or on television or radio, including the sentence, to show how it was being used.

- During the sessions, the tutor and learner can work on these words.

c) Don't overload

For the learner to develop a rich reading vocabulary, it is important to:

- Work on vocabulary each session.
- Limit direct vocabulary instruction to 5 –10 words per session.
- Balance it with the other elements of reading.

d) Ensure repeated use

To remember new words, learners need to see and use them repeatedly. This experience can include any or all of the four language forms of listening, speaking, reading and writing.

e) Vary the approaches

Combine teaching word definitions with other strategies. Learners will remember better when vocabulary activities are fun and interesting.

For example:

- Word games and jokes can keep repeated use from getting tiresome.
- The tutor can construct activities using puns, homophones, synonyms, and antonyms.
- Many vocabulary activities and games are available on the Internet. For example, native speakers, as well as English as a Second Language learners, can enjoy the site "Dave's ESL Café," at http://eslcafe.com/search/Vocabulary/index.html.

f) Provide sensory experience

A range of senses will provide especially vivid experiences. For example:

- Learners could learn the names of exotic vegetables and fruits by using them in a recipe with the tutor, if practical, or they could feel, smell and taste them at the session.
- Names of engine parts could be learned by looking under the hood of a car.
- Printed matter such as cookbooks and owners' manuals with illustrations can be used afterwards to make the connection with the words in print.

g) See relationships between words

Understanding how new words relate to one another helps a learner grasp meanings and remember them later.

- The foods or engine parts mentioned above can be thought of in relation to one another.

- The tutor or learner could draw pictures or charts demonstrating these relationships.

III. WORD IDENTIFICATION: LEARNING TO READ WORDS

Readers have to be able to recognize words in print. This can be done by memorizing the whole word, by putting together sounds of letters or groups of letters, or both, aided by the reader's expectation of what would make sense.

A. Recognizing Words by Sight

The first words people learn to read, such as their own names, are usually learned as wholes. This way of learning words is useful for many words, so we will present some of these words, along with strategies for recognizing them by sight.

When good readers are reading about familiar subjects, they recognize most of the words quickly. The best way for new readers to develop a large sight vocabulary is to read as much as possible, learning to recognize words by seeing them repeatedly in context, in the same way that word meanings were picked up.

However, if the reader keeps having trouble with some words, the easiest way to learn them may be to memorize them by sight, as whole words.

1. Which are the most useful words to know by sight?

It is useful to know the words the learner is likely to run into. The New Instant Word List, shown in Appendix 1, consists of the hundred words most frequently used in print. Many of the words on this list will already be known by learners because they have been seen so many times, but the list is useful for finding words which come up often and give trouble every time. The list was made by Edward Fry, who counted words that appeared in publications such as newspapers and books in 1980.

2. Why are these words best learned by sight?

Many of these words need an extra effort to learn for one or more of these reasons:
- They are spelled irregularly, and so are hard to decode by the sounds of the letters (though).

- They resemble other words (were and where).
- Their meanings cannot be visualized (of, about).
- The learner's own learning experiences.

3. How can these words be learned?

Although words are recognized at sight they may need to be learned by using senses other than sight because different people learn in different ways. For example, a person might learn to get somewhere by looking at a map, by listening to someone give directions, by tracing on the map with a finger, or by remembering how it felt to go there. Words, too, may be learned through any of the four senses. Learners can experiment to see which of these approaches works best for them:

- Visual – – remembering what they see.
- Aural – – remembering what they hear.
- Kinesthetic – – learning from how they use their muscles.
- Tactile – – learning through their sense of touch.

a) Visual-auditory (seeing and hearing)

Flash cards are one of the most familiar ways to memorize the more common irregularly written words. Words can be put on flash cards and practiced with a helper, and then independently. Many people have used flash cards for memorization of multiplication facts or words in a language they are learning. One of the advantages of flash cards is that a learner can use them independently, learning and self-testing by looking at the answers as needed. This is the procedure:

- The tutor and learner make flash cards for some known words, doubtful words, and unknown words.
- They choose a set of about ten cards, some from each group.
- The learner or tutor reads each word aloud, after which the student says it again and makes a mental picture of it, with eyes closed.
- The learner reads the words in the pile again, putting the ones that are remembered in one pile, and those that are not in another.
- The learner works again on the words that were not remembered, reading them with help, and saying the words while visualizing them.

This is another use of flash cards for a learner who knows very few words:

- The tutor makes a card for every word in a sentence that a learner is trying to read.
- The learner reads the sentence in the story, then reads the cards arranged by the tutor in the same order.

- The tutor mixes the cards up and lets the learner put them in the same order and read them again.

b) Tactile-visual-auditory (touching, seeing and hearing)

For this method, the tutor writes a word on any convenient surface that can be felt with the fingertips.

- It can be on fabric, punched onto styrofoam with a pin or the point of a knife, or traced on flour on a table.
- The learner reads the word aloud while tracing it with his finger.

c) Kinesthetic-visual-auditory (moving, seeing and hearing)

The learner writes the word in the air, copying from a paper, while saying it.

- The learner may also write the word in large letters on paper with a marker while saying it aloud.

What are some other word learning activities?

- The learner writes sentences with the words being studied.
- The learner circles the words in a newspaper article, dictated story, or other book of interest.
- Concentration game: This is especially good for small groups.
  1. Two flash cards are made for each word, for 5-10 words.
  2. The cards are shuffled and placed face down in rows on the table.
  3. Learners take turns turning two cards over at a time, trying to get a match.
  4. Learners read the cards they turn over.
  5. If the cards match and are read correctly, the learner keeps the pair.
  6. The winner is the person with the most pairs at the end of the game.

B. Decoding Letters into Sounds

Many of the adult literacy learners who can read very few things, and some who read fairly well recognizing words by sight and context, are unable to decode, or "sound out" unfamiliar words even when they are spelled in predictable ways. Most learners know the alphabet, the names of the letters, and the sounds of most of the consonants, but they may have gaps in their knowledge of the sounds of certain letters or combinations, or they may have trouble applying the knowledge they have to their reading.

For these adult literacy learners, the information in this section may be helpful in filling in gaps in their knowledge or getting practice in applying what they know to new words. They may need help with hearing sounds (phonemic awareness) or with matching sounds and letters (phonics).

1. Phonemic awareness: Hearing the sounds

To begin with the smallest units of language, readers need to be able to hear individual sounds or phonemes before they can use them as a reading aid. A phoneme is a single sound which may be spelled with one letter, or more than one letter, such as /ch/ or /ai/.

Learners with little experience with the printed page tend to have trouble with sorting out these separate sounds in words. Native speakers of other languages who are not literate in their own language, or whose written language, like many Asian languages, is not based on sounds, may have similar difficulty. Learners may benefit from some of the exercises in this section as preparation for learning the sounds of letters.

How does a tutor teach awareness of sounds? A tutor can provide exercises to help learners isolate and distinguish the sounds within a word. For example, mail, (which happens to have four letters) has 3 sounds, or phonemes, /m/ /ay/ /l/. Letters between slashes should be read as sounds, not letters.

The following exercises, with any short word, can help a learner become aware of the sounds in words:
- Counting: How many sounds are there in "pig?"
- Isolating: What is the first sound in "car?"
- Segmenting: What are the sounds in "cup?"
- Blending: What word does /b/ /l/ /a/ /k/ make?
- Substituting: What would you have if "tail" started with /n/?

Various materials can make the activities more interesting or memorable:
- Playing the game of Concentration, described in the previous section, in which the tutor lays out, face down, pairs of pictures which share a common sound (beginning, middle, or final). Players take turns trying to turn up two cards with the same sound.
- Counting sounds by tapping on the table with a pencil.
- Substituting sounds by making up short rhymed poems, including rap lines with a rhyme in the middle of the line.

2. Phonics

What is phonics? Phonics is the study of how letters are used to represent the sounds of the language. Traditionally, this has been done by focusing on one or two letters at a time. Single consonants are usually studied first, followed by consonant blends, /bl/ or /st/, and then digraphs, such as /th/ and /sh/. Vowels, being more variable, are taught next: first the short sounds, as in cat and hop, then the long ones, as in came and goat. While workbooks and flash cards are available for traditional phonics, we recommend the patterns approach, which teaches the sounds of letters as they occur in words.

3. Sound/spelling patterns or "word families"

a) What are sound/spelling patterns?

Sound/spelling patterns, often referred to as "word families," are groups of letters that occur in predictable patterns, such as the *-ig* in *big, pig,* and *wig,* or *-ight* in *night, fight* and *tight.*

b) How is the patterns approach different from traditional phonics?

The patterns approach begins instruction with patterns made by groups of letters in words, rather than with isolated sounds. Learners arrive at their own idea of sounds and letters inductively by seeing many examples in similarly spelled words, such as cat, or big.

c) Why is this more effective? It offers these advantages:

- Patterns of several letters are easier to hear than individual letter sounds. When we say letter sounds in isolation, and then try to put them together in a word, we give an unnatural sound to each letter, as in "kuh-a-tuh," for cat.

- One pattern can be the basic building block for learning many other words. By changing initial consonants or consonant blends, for example: *cap* leads to *nap, map, rap,* or to *slap, clap,* and *snap.* With the endings changed: *cap* leads to *can, camp, cash.*

d) What about differences in pronunciation?

Every reader has the challenge of matching print with his or her own speech patterns. Regional accents sometimes affect whether words with the same spelling patterns do or don't sound alike. But even if a speaker might pronounce the *o* in *dog* differently from *hog, log,* and *frog,* the pattern can still be learned for the words that do fit.

e) How are word spelling patterns taught?

A learner who knows the names of the letters but cannot decode unfamiliar words can start noticing common patterns this way:

- The tutor makes a list, starting with a word the student already knows, and following it with words of the same spelling pattern whose first letter sounds like the name of the letter:

>   big
>
>   pig
>
>   dig
>
>   fig

- The tutor asks the learner to read the first word, then the second word, noting that it looks and sounds like the other one except that it begins with *p*.

- If the student has trouble, the tutor asks, "Do you hear the sound of the letter *p* in the word *pig*?" The student reads the next word, with the tutor naming the initial letter, then saying the word if necessary, and the next.

- The tutor asks the student to add to the list, saying "Can you think of other words that sound like this?"

- The student might think of *rig*, and *wig*. The tutor would point out the sound of /w/, noting that it does not sound like its own letter name.

- The student reads the list aloud, first in order, then from the bottom up, then reading the words the tutors asks for, then in random order as the tutor points to different words.

By changing the consonants, the tutor is reminding the student of the sound of those initial letters, and at the same time teaching the *-ig* pattern. Sounds of letters are taught by example as they occur in words, rather than in isolation. They are much easier to remember this way.

Similar lists can be made for other patterns, including unusual spellings:

>   night
>
>   light
>
>   tight
>
>   right
>
>   sight

C. Looking at Word Parts

1. Separating into syllables

Learners often are intimidated by long words which they could read if they looked at them one syllable at a time. Often by the time the learner has figured out the first syllable or two, the meaning of the sentence will bring the word to mind.

Many syllables fall into familiar patterns, such as:

can	did	ate		
ter	ri	ble		
sat	is	fac	tion	
in	ter	na	tion	al

Each syllable in a word makes one sound, spelled by at least one vowel, (except for the silent *e* in *ble*) and it usually has a consonant on one or both sides of it, as in the examples above. The dictionary tells how to divide each word when necessary in writing, but for recognizing a word, the tutor can use her own judgment.

The tutor and learner could practice reading long words this way:

- The tutor writes the word, then covers all but the first syllable with a small piece of paper.
- After the learner reads it, with help if needed, the tutor uncovers the next syllable, and so on, until the word is pronounced.
- After a few words read this way, the tutor could write another word, and lightly pencil in slash marks between each syllable, and let the learner try it.
- Later, the learner could try penciling in the slash marks and reading the word on his own.

2. Seeing beginnings and endings

Beginnings, or prefixes, and endings, or suffixes, are extremely useful in decoding many words. When the learner can see common prefixes and suffixes separately from the main part, or root, many words will be easier to recognize, such as:

un-   To help a learner recognize these parts, the tutor
dis-   and the learner can make their own lists of words
over-   whose beginnings or endings gave difficulty.
anti-

and

-tion
-able
-less
-ly

3. Seeing the Parts of Compound Words

Analyzing compound words, or two words written as one, is another way of looking at word parts. A learner who is unable to recognize *watermelon* or *overpass,* will be able to read it when he realizes that it is made up of two familiar words. Here are two ways to get experience with seeing words within words:

- The tutor helps a learner by asking, "Do you see two smaller words in this word?"
- Tutors and learners could practice recognizing compound words by putting together a short list of their own examples.

IV. SOME QUESTIONS AND ANSWERS ABOUT READING

These answers to questions often asked by tutors or learners may provide useful reminders or supplementary information:

Q: My learner skips lines when reading text. What can I do to help?

A: Encourage your learner to use a tracking device, such as: an index card, their finger, a pencil, or a tracking bar which can be purchased.

Q: If a learner has a very hard time remembering new material from one week to the next, what can we do about it?

A: There are several strategies that you can use to help your student remember information.

1. Use mnemonic tricks. For example, "When two vowels go walking, the first does the talking."
2. Frequently review skills and provide ample opportunity for practice.
3. Connect new learning to old knowledge.
4. Provide written information that the learner can use as a reference.

Q: If a person sometimes reads words backwards, does that mean he's dyslexic?

A: Reading words backwards is not a sign of dyslexia. Reversals of words, such as confusing *was* and *saw,* or *on* and *no,* can be the result of inexperience. Reading words in the meaningful context of stories will reduce this type of error. Additional strategies that you can use to help are:

1. Emphasizing instruction for one over the other. For instance, focus on teaching the word *was.*
2. Emphasizing reading from left to right.

3. Encouraging learner to use a tracking device.

4. Providing a memory clue.

Q: My learner said that he has dyslexia. What is dyslexia and how do I help this learner?

A: Experts in the field of reading do not have an agreed upon definition of dyslexia. In general, dyslexia is the inability to process written symbols. The teaching strategies provided in this manual are effective in helping adults with dyslexia.

Q: My learner told me that she has a learning disability. What does that mean and what can I do to help?

A: There are many forms of learning disabilities. For example, many people have a hard time telling left from right or remembering numbers unless they have seen them written down. Some people have a terrible time learning how to spell. While a learning disability makes learning harder, there are usually ways around the difficulty. If a person has learned to read and write anything at all, such as her own name, then she is able to learn to read and write something. The teaching strategies provided in this manual are effective in helping adults with learning disabilities. The challenge is to find out which approaches work best for your particular learner. Just remember to be patient with yourself and your learner.

Q: My learner would like to be evaluated to see if he has a learning disability. What steps should he take to have that happen? Would that diagnosis be beneficial to him?

A: A certified psychologist can provide an official diagnosis of a learning disability. A diagnosis is provided after the learner participates in a battery of tests, and the psychologist interprets the results. However, this is a costly process for a literacy organization or an individual to take on and is not always necessary.

An official diagnosis is only necessary for providing accommodations on standardized testing, such as the GED or college entrance exams, or receiving accommodations at a place of employment. However, an official diagnosis is not required for a learner to be successful in a literacy program. The tutor and the learner need to be aware of the learner's strengths and weaknesses and be able to find strategies for success.

Q: The people in my group are at different levels. How can we work on reading together without some being bored and others feeling left behind?

A: Learners of different reading levels can learn together by doing the following:

- Learners can use the same materials together, in a group, using different techniques, according to their ability, such as the more proficient students reading aloud to the others, and the less proficient ones doing echo reading or following along as another person reads aloud.

- More advanced learners are taught how to supply less able readers with words:

  One person is designated as the helper.

  Readers are given a moment to figure out unknown words.

  Misreadings that do not affect the meaning are not corrected.

- After group oral reading, everyone rereads the piece silently.
- Regardless of reading ability, everyone can build comprehension skills. Together, they can discuss the meaning, importance, or believability of what was read together.
- Less proficient readers use the language experience approach by dictating stories to the tutor or to another learner while the others are doing in-class writing.
- All the learners choose their own materials to read independently at home, periodically summarizing and telling the others about what they are reading.

Q: Isn't it a waste of time to read silently during the tutoring sessions?

A: It is good for learners to read silently during their sessions so they can talk about and practice comprehension strategies. For instance, they need to be reminded about the importance of going back and rereading if things stop making sense. Don't worry about the fact that the tutor does not hear the learners read every word, because getting every word right is less important than understanding the meaning from what can be read.

V. CONCLUSION: PUTTING THE PARTS TOGETHER AGAIN

Newly learned things are easily forgotten unless they are used often and in an interesting way, engaging the learner's attention. Reading goal-related material is the best review of vocabulary, word recognition, letter sounds and word parts. Writing, discussed in the next chapter, is another way to apply newly learned reading knowledge.

Chapter 5

Writing

This chapter will show how to give learners a tool to meet their literacy needs and to experience the satisfaction of expressing themselves on paper.

I. ABOUT LEARNING TO WRITE

A. What is Writing?

As we have said earlier, writing is one of the elements of literacy, along with reading and the ability to use numbers. While a reader creates meaning from print by looking at it, a writer creates meaning by putting the print on the page. Writing, like speech, produces language, while reading, like listening, involves receiving it.

The act of writing can be very satisfying, just as talking is satisfying, because the writer is in charge of what goes on the page. For the writer, writing can meet many needs, both practical and emotional. These include writing for themselves, for recording, reflecting, and problem-solving, as well as communicating with others to share thoughts and feelings or to convince them to do something.

While it is satisfying, getting words on paper is harder work than talking, and can carry more risk than either speaking or reading because unlike speech, what is written stays there for all to see.

B. Why Work on Writing Along with Reading?

Even though tutors and learners may want to put off writing for later after working on reading, because it seems more difficult, there are many reasons for doing both at the same time, regardless of the level of the learner. Working on the two together helps both writing and reading at the word level as well as with comprehension.

- When people write, they put to use and remember the skills they are developing as readers because the physical act of writing is a powerful memory aid.
- When people become writers themselves, they become more perceptive readers, able to see the writer's point of view more easily.

- Learners get additional experience in reading as they reread their own work.
- Reading helps people learn the mechanics of writing: spelling, punctuation, and sentence structure which they see repeatedly.

- Reading supports writing by modeling ways of saying things and providing ideas to write about.

C. The Balanced Literacy Approach to Writing Instruction

We recommend focusing on a balanced approach, as we did for reading, of the elements of writing: **producing**, in which the writer looks mostly inward, for what to say, and **polishing**, which involves looking outward to the reader, to decide how to say it. This chapter will present ways to work on both phases: getting words on the page and looking over those words for the sake of the future readers.

We can think of writers as going through five stages. The first two, planning and drafting, are parts of the productive phase; in the next three, revising, editing and proof-reading, the writer evaluates and improves at all levels. It is wise to keep the two phases of producing and evaluating separate, and concentrate on the producing first. If a writer starts criticizing her work too soon, very little gets written.

These are the five stages:

1. Planning: Deciding on a topic, collecting information. "What do I want to say?"

2. Drafting: Putting the ideas and information down on paper. The writer gets the words on the page, expressing thoughts and feelings without self-evaluation.

3. Revising: Looking at the ideas; "Is this what I wanted to say? Is it true? Does it make sense?"

4. Editing: Trying to see it through the eyes of the future reader, looking at the style, and whether it is clearly written, well-organized, and how the words and sentences sound; "Did I say it the way I wanted to? Will they listen? Will they get it?"

5. Proofreading: Making sure it is free of distracting mistakes in sentence structure, spelling, and punctuation. "Did I do it right?"

While this progression from the first idea to the finished product looks orderly, in real life the process is messier. Writers often move back and forth, making changes at all stages of the process. People might revise, edit and proofread as they draft, and draft or plan again as a result of revision. Still, having an idea of these stages may keep new writers from getting stuck on self-evaluation before they've generated enough ideas.

It is also true that not every writing task requires all these stages. All writing requires drafting, and most writing takes at least some planning, but how much revising, editing and proofreading to do will depend on many things, including the purpose for writing and who will be reading it.

The tutor's role progresses through these stages:

- Helping think of ideas in the producing phases.
- Responding to the ideas after the draft is written.
- Asking or suggesting during the revising and editing, where the learner makes choices.
- Direct teaching in the proofreading stages, where the learner might need information.

Section IIC, "Helping the Learner Go Through the Process," presents strategies for helping the learner at different stages.

D. How Do People Improve at Writing?

The needs of literacy learners for writing are similar to those for reading:

1. Writing activities that are important and relevant to them

The most effective writing learners can do is for an authentic purpose rather than simply for practice. The purpose could be as simple as making a shopping list, or it could be a letter to a newspaper on an issue the writer cares deeply about.

2. Writing with someone who can make the task easier and provide helpful feedback

The tutor's role is to make the producing phase easier and to provide reactions, suggestions and information during the refining phase.

This includes:

- Helping the writer get started by discussing goals, purpose, and audience.
- Making the activity comfortable for the learner by writing at the same time and emphasizing ideas before correctness.
- Making writing easy for the learner with instructional strategies (see Section IIB).
- Responding to the ideas expressed.
- Helping put the ideas in a form that is appropriate for the purpose and the future reader.

3. Lots of experience doing it

Writers need "mileage," as they say of people learning to ski. This is best accomplished by including writing in every tutoring session and at home as well.

E. Writing and the Adult Learner

People who learn to read and write as adults may have had very little experience writing. They might have avoided it because they didn't enjoy it, working out alternatives such as using the telephone or relying on an excellent memory. As a result, learners may have never thought much about using writing as a way of expressing themselves, getting things done, or any of its other purposes. Tutors can help learners experience these advantages.

Learners may also have a limited view of the writing process. Their experiences with spelling tests, penmanship, and grammar exercises may have given them an idea of revising as being mainly focused on correctness in grammar, spelling and punctuation. Many learners believe that good writers get it right the first time, not realizing that most writing for others to read involves making changes that go beyond correcting errors. Tutors can help learners understand that rewriting is a normal part of the writing process, help learners focus on their purpose and audience, and see the value of rethinking, clarifying, and rephrasing.

Adult learners may feel fearful about writing, remembering all the red pencil marks on their school papers. They may avoid writing in front of other people for fear of the embarrassment of spelling words wrong or the poor appearance of their handwriting. They may feel very uncomfortable if they have to write a letter to their children's school or complete paperwork related to their job. Tutors can do many things to reduce this anxiety.

II. WORKING TOGETHER ON WRITING

A. What to Write? Finding Activities that Meet Learners' Goals

In this section, we describe what a learner might write, with tips on how the tutor can help. We will discuss personal writing, both practical and self-expressive; writing for others, either to entertain or persuade them; and finally, essay writing for academic purposes, including the GED test and college entrance exams.

There are many reasons or purposes for writing, so a learner has a wide range of choices of what to write about. The Goals Checklist is a good place to start, as many learner goals relate to writing. Another is simply to brainstorm together, making a list of all the reasons they might want to write something.

Questions on purpose and audience: Along with deciding what to write about, it helps to think about questions like these:

Why is the piece being written?

> to record and remember?
>
> to share with others?
>
> to vent feelings?
>
> to solve a problem?
>
> to maintain a relationship?
>
> to get something done?

Who is going to read it?

> the writer?
>
> the person it will be sent to?
>
> the audience at an event such as the Student Speak Out events mentioned in Chapter 3?
>
> a test examiner or college admissions counselors?
>
> a possible employer?

1. Personal writing

Ordinary life tasks and journal writing provide adult learners with writing experience while meeting their personal needs. The tutor and learner can decide how much revising to do, depending on who besides the writer will be reading these materials.

a) Writing to meet practical needs:

Many learners come for help with everyday writing tasks related to their daily needs. If the learner's Goals Checklist shows that she wants to look for a job, for example, she may want to work on job applications and a resumé.

Doing these tasks provides a more powerful learning experience when it is real. The learner should use the actual materials, such as applications, and pass them on to the appropriate reader.

A learner might choose from these:

- shopping lists
- notes to self, family, school
- catalogue orders
- forms (application for job, loan, school, health records)
- résumés
- letters to friends and relatives

b) Journals: private thoughts.

People can use journals for recording their thoughts, experiences and feelings, to solve their problems, or to vent their feelings. No one has to read the journal except the writer. Writing without the fear of failure or criticism encourages self-confidence and gives the learner experience in the

first two stages, pre-writing and drafting, where many writers get stuck, going into the self-evaluation phases of writing too early.

Here are some guidelines for journal writing during sessions:

- The tutor should provide help only when asked, answering quickly to avoid interrupting the flow of thought and writing.

- Learners can also make up a spelling for the moment and be reminded that errors are not important in journal writing, since the only reader may be themselves.

- Ten minutes for journal writing in a tutoring session works well for most people.

- Learners will have an easier time writing if the tutors write too. They can share writing or not, as they choose.

Journal writing also lends itself to writing outside of tutoring sessions. Learners have a chance to express themselves and to become better writers through practice. Ten minutes two or three times a week is fine, and the entries do not have to be long. The greatest benefit is in writing regularly because the time will add up.

What can you put in a journal?

Anything. A journal is personal and doesn't have to please anybody but the writer. He just needs to get something on paper. Here are some suggestions:

- What happened today and how you feel about it.

- Start like this to get your thoughts moving:

    I feel stuck today. I really

    I don't have time to write much today because

- Write a response to things read recently, as described in the next section.

- See Appendix 2, section III, for a list, "50 Journal Topics," for ideas for journal or other writing. This list, along with spaces for recording the number of minutes, words and date, can give the learner a sense of progress by seeing the changes in amount of writing over time.

Journals shared between learner and tutor

Many learners and tutors like communicating with each other through a journal written by the learner, which the tutor reads later and responds to by writing in the same book. Dialogue journals provide an opportunity for learners and tutors to interact with each other about things they don't get to during tutoring sessions.

Learners and tutors look forward to reading each other's responses. As learners become used to writing and less worried about making errors, they start to enjoy it and to write more often.

Here are some recommendations for using dialogue journals:

- Tutors and learners can keep two journal books going, so that the learner will have a book to give the tutor at each meeting, without having to wait to get the first one back.

- The tutor can encourage additional writing on topics by asking questions which inspire more communication.

- Rather than correcting the learner's writing, the tutor teaches by modeling correct writing and spelling in her responses.

- The tutor lists on a separate paper any writing skills that could be taught opportunistically.

2. Reaching a wider audience

a) Letters and reports

These are an important writing need for literacy learners who want to communicate with people elsewhere other than by telephone. How much revising and help the learner will need depends on the learner's skills, the purpose of the letter, and who will be reading it. An informal style is fine for social letters, but learners will probably need help revising, editing and proofreading in order to get favorable attention from businesses, news editors, or public officials.

Learners should be encouraged to send any letters that are written. They can be for many purposes and audiences, including:

- Cover letters to go with résumés, asking for a job.
- Letters to organizations or businesses requesting help or change in policy.
- Letters to newspaper editors expressing strongly felt opinions.
- Letters asking a question from a newspaper feature such as "Dear Abby."
- A letter with questions or comments to the author of a recently read book (send it to the publisher).
- Reports at work.
- Minutes of meetings.

b) Essays, stories, or poems, for possible publication

People often start writing to express their thoughts and feelings for themselves, but after they are finished, decide they would enjoy having their words read by others. Publications by literacy organizations provide adult learners with this opportunity. Learners can get ideas for writing by reading examples of student-written poems, short stories, and personal opinion pieces, as described in Chapter 3.

Here are two pieces, an opinion piece and a poem, that Center for Literacy learners wrote for the Student Speak Out event and publication:

Why I Am Going to Vote
by Laura Calder

I am voting because it is important for me to let others know what I am for or against, rather than sit back and allow others to lead me in directions I choose not to go. It is also important to allow all others to voice their opinions and beliefs as they do likewise to me. To remain silent and offer nothing, one gets nothing in return.

People who don't vote do so because they don't want to get involved, and blame the world's problems on everyone but themselves. There are people who care about how the world does, while those who care about nothing reap nothing of value. I may not care about the candidates personally, but I am concerned about their business, which is me, you and everyone.

ME
by Kyssandra B. Frye
As I stare into the stars and the heavens above
I think of beautiful spring days and summer nights I've loved.
I think of the days gone by and of the days to come,
But mostly I think of me, and all that I've become.
I've grown up from a baby covered with frilly lace
I've grown from that child with a chubby face
I've grown up from a little girl with every fall
I've grown into an adult and I feel I have it all!

Poetry: Poems are fun because they can be short, and you make up your own rules. Learners should be reminded that poems don't have to rhyme, although many learners enjoy rhyming for the challenge of doing it and the way it sounds.

Reading can be combined with writing when learners get ideas from reading student work like the one above or from reading published poets:

- Adult learners have enjoyed the work of Robert Frost, Langston Hughes, Carl Sandburg, William Carlos Williams, Maya Angelou, Nikki Giovanni, and Emily Dickinson.
- Well-known poems and songs are easy to find on the Internet.
- Since the poems learners write tend to be short, the tutor could word process the poems written in one session, for reading in the next.

Getting started: There are several ways a tutor can help a learner get started on poems, essays or stories:

- The tutor and learner could brainstorm ideas together.
- Learners could look in their own journals for ideas to expand on.
- Learners should focus first on getting the ideas on paper, without self-criticism.
- This kind of writing is easier for the learner if the tutor writes too.

Getting ideas from books and newspapers: Besides writing letters to newspapers and authors, learners could write the following:

- A story, poem or opinion piece inspired by something in a book or a newspaper.
- Their own ending for a story in a book, before or after finishing it.
- An imaginary letter to one of the characters in the story.
- A poem following the pattern and/or subject of one they read.

More ideas: Appendix 2 offers some scenes to help learners write stories or poems based on their own experience and imagination.

c) Family history: to record the past

Learners might want to interview and write about older family members or friends for stories that they remember from the past. Often, in discussing memories or experiences, someone will speak of a lesson that he learned or a story he heard. In talking about his family's history of work, one man remembered his grandmother's midwifery and her reputation for having more skill than the local doctor. Stories such as this should be preserved before the storyteller passes on.

The learner, with the tutor's support, can plan the interview:

- Choose a person to interview.

- Plan and write down interview questions.

- Bring a pen and paper for taking notes during the interview, writing down key words and phrases for important and interesting points.

3. Essays for GED and college: Writing for an academic setting

Some learners want to be able to successfully write for academic purposes. Many learners have an interest in passing their GED Essay exam, while others wish to complete the essay portion of a college application.

a) What is an essay?

An essay is a general statement of an idea or opinion, supported by reasons and explanations. In an academic setting, an essay is judged by its depth and originality, its reasoning or logic, its structure and organization, its clarity of style, and its conformity to the conventions of writing, including sentence structure, punctuation and spelling.

Essays can take many forms, including these:

- Narrative: in which a story supports the point made in the beginning.

- Descriptive: in which an overall impression is supported by sensory images.

- Persuasive: in which an opinion is defended from the reader's disagreement.

- Cause and effect: which explains why something happens.

- Compare and contrast: in which two things are shown to be different in some ways, alike in others.

- Process: which is an explanation of how something is done or happens.

The writing part of the GED test requires an essay expressing an opinion on some topic. The writer is expected to state an opinion, or make a thesis statement, in the first paragraph, followed by several paragraphs, each developing a reason, or an example, to support this opinion. The final paragraph is expected to summarize the examples and relate them back to the opinion. GED workbooks and college writing texts give examples of this type of essay.

b) What is a paragraph?

Learners also need to know about paragraphs, which make reading easier by grouping information in logical, predictable order. Starting a new paragraph signals "new idea coming up." The easiest kind of paragraph to read contains one main idea that is stated at the beginning and proved or explained in the sentences that follow. A paragraph is like a miniature version of an essay. It starts with a topic sentence, supported by other sentences, instead of the essay's thesis paragraph supported by other paragraphs. A paragraph usually closes with a sentence that summarizes or qualifies the main idea or prepares for the next paragraph. Not all paragraphs are built like this in real life, but such a structure makes an essay clearer.

c) How do you develop a thesis for an essay?

To write an essay, tutors and learners can use any topic in which they have a strong interest. They need to collect information, organize it, and develop an idea about it. The next section of this chapter on the writing process describes the planning of an essay about the late reggae singer Bob Marley.

B. Ways to Make Challenging Writing Easier

As we have said, learners make progress when doing work that is challenging, but not frustrating. The tutor's role is to help find the right level of difficulty and provide support. Tutors can help by having learners try one or more of the following four strategies: dictating, copying, sentence completion and free writing. They are listed in order of how supportive they are. The first two of these activities are excellent for very new writers; others are helpful for more experienced learners who are writing something very challenging. The last, free writing, is helpful no matter how experienced the writer is.

1. Dictating to the tutor

Telling a story, or dictating a letter, for someone else to write down is helpful to a new writer who has an idea but feels intimidated about spelling or even forming letters. The strategy of learners dictating their own stories to the tutor is described in Chapter 3, under "Learner-Dictated Materials," because student-dictated stories make such excellent beginning level reading material. But the learner should be reminded that the most important aspect of writing is expressing your ideas, and how it gets onto paper is secondary. Dictating a story is actually the producing stage of writing, using the help of a secretary.

Here is a reminder of what to do:

- The story need not be long; a quarter of a page is fine.
- The tutor writes the learner's exact words.
- The tutor prints clearly, skipping every other line.
- The learner and tutor can then read the story, together, getting the benefits of combining reading and writing.
- At the same session or next time, the learner can do the writing, either copying the story, or writing a new story with many of the same words.

There are more detailed instructions in Chapter 3, under "Learner-Dictated Materials."

2. Copying

This is almost as supported an activity as dictating and is very helpful to writers with very little experience. Imagine trying to write Chinese for the first time. No doubt you would give great attention to every single stroke of your pen. And, no doubt, you would find it very helpful to copy the Chinese symbols until you could make them correctly and independently. While most adult learners already know the shapes and names of the letters, new writers often welcome the opportunity to practice forming letters by copying.

When learners copy interesting or important material, so that they think about what they are writing, they get experience writing and reading whole words and sentences as well as practice in forming letters. Copying gives learners experience in writing sentences correctly, exposing them to punctuation and spelling patterns.

Another benefit of copying is that it lets new writers exercise the muscles in the hand associated with writing. New writers often report that writing hurts their hands, the way it might bother a person who had to write after she got used to using a word processor. Copying allows new writers to develop these muscles in a non-stressful way.

These are useful for copying:

- Materials related to learner goals.
- Familiar materials such as favorite poems, song lyrics or Bible verses.
- Emergency telephone numbers and addresses.
- Dictated language experience pieces, especially letters to send to family members or friends.

3. Completing sentences

This technique helps new writers get started by suggesting an idea in the first part of a sentence and inviting them to finish it. Sentence completion exercises enable students to express important thoughts, feelings and ideas in writing, often for the first time in their lives. Because they are working on just single sentences, the task does not seem formidable.

Here are some examples; the tutor could make up others:

- I want _____
- When I am sixty-five_____
- I believe _____
- My hardest decision was to _____
- I hate_____
- If I could change one thing about my town _____
- I am proud that _____
- I hope my children will _____

Below are samples of sentences written by learners. Notice how much even the most simply worded sentence can convey.

- I believe in God.
- I hate nobody.
- I hope my children will be happy.

4. Free writing

Like journal writing, free writing allows the learner to put words on paper without the worry of doing it right. It can be used by more experienced writers as well as inexperienced ones. It gets people into writing but bypasses the planning stage, jumping right into drafting and writing anything that comes to mind, usually without a topic. The goal is to write as much as possible in a short period of time.

For new writers, the emphasis on speed rather than correctness focuses them on producing as much as they can. Often they are surprised at how much they were able to write. If they manage to invent the spelling of unknown words, they benefit by matching sounds and letters as they hear them.

For more experienced writers, free writing gets them to write fluently and overcome writer's block. It can serve as the planning phase for a longer piece, including finding a topic, and it also allows the writer to record an assortment of ideas to be picked over and organized later.

It's easier for the learner when the tutor writes too. This is how to do it:

- Get a pencil or pen and some blank paper. A timer is useful, too.
- Decide whether or not you want a topic, and if so, pick one.
- Decide how long to write (five to ten minutes) and check the time.
- Begin writing and write continuously.
- If you can't think of anything to say, write the same words, or how you feel about not being able to think of anything.
- If you don't know how spell a word, make up a spelling, put down the first letter only, or leave it blank.
- Stop when the time is up.
- The tutor and learner can share their writing or not, as they choose.

Once learners get used to it, they usually enjoy free writing. They begin to experience the pleasure of self-expression, with the tutor providing a model. Positive experiences with pencil and paper help the learners think of themselves as writers.

C. Helping the Learner Go Through the Process

This section describes the five stages of the writing process in more detail and gives recommendations for how the tutor can help at each stage. As we have said earlier, going through the stages of planning, drafting, revising, editing, and proofreading is often a back and forth process, but it is easier to think about them in this sequence.

We describe strategies for planning, ways of responding to first drafts, ways to get a writer to think about revising, questions to ask while editing, and techniques for proofreading. Since the editing and proofreading stages often provide the tutor with useful feedback on skills the learner may need to develop, this section also describes ways to take time out to address what kind of English the writer wants to use and examples of opportunistic teaching of spelling and punctuation which encourage learners to see patterns and rules for themselves.

1. Planning

Once the purpose and task have been established, the writer can begin planning what to write. Pre-drafting activities help writers get started and give them an idea of what they will be saying. To help learners get started, tutors can encourage learners to do one or more of these activities:

- Writing questions to be answered.
- Gathering information by reading.
- Gathering information by talking to people.
- Brainstorming: listing everything you can think of about a topic.
- Free, or non-stop writing.
- Grouping items in different lists.
- Making an outline.
- Making an idea map.

What is an idea map? An idea map is like an outline, but it is more free-flowing, because it works out in all directions from the middle of the page, rather than down from the top. It provides freedom for collecting ideas, without having to put them in order yet. The main idea is represented in a box or bubble in the center, while supporting ideas are placed in bubbles or boxes around it like a miniature solar system. Details are placed around the supporting ideas. After the map is drawn, the main points can be numbered in the order the writer wants them.

Suppose you want to write about the importance of learning logs. You could write "Learning Log" in a circle in the center of a page, and then list the different aspects you wanted to explain on lines branching out from the center. The idea map might look something like this.

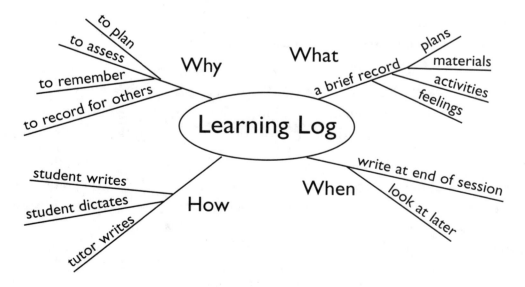

There is no single right way to do it. You just need to do what makes sense to you. This activity demonstrates the fact that writing is really a thinking process. Making a concept map is not only a useful tool for writing but can be used as a memory aid when reading.

For a longer piece, such as an essay, the learner might use the planning stage to organize the information and to find what the main point, or thesis, will be. This could be done by making an idea map, or an outline, as in the example below:

Suppose that a writer wants to write an essay about the life of late reggae musician Bob Marley. The learner needs to find a main idea, or thesis, for the essay, so he begins by brainstorming, with help from the tutor, the following list of words and phrases suggesting information about the subject:

reggae musician	from Jamaica
famous black person	was Rastafarian
smoked marijuana	sang about love
believed marijuana was healthy	many Americans learned about Jamaica
first popular reggae musician	most important reggae musician
inspiring songs	many people copied his musical style
influential to blacks and others	marijuana important to Rastafarian religion
had lots of kids by lots of women	songs about society overcoming racism
sang of poor people fighting for rights	people became Rastafarians

The learner can group the ideas in a rough outline, with the more general idea at the top of each group, and related specific facts underneath, as follows:

Reggae musician – first and most important
Famous and influential black person

Jamaica
        Helped people there
        Made Americans aware of

Smoked marijuana
        Advocated smoking marijuana
        Believed that smoking marijuana was good for health and spirit

Was Rastafarian
        Many Americans and others then became Rastafarians

Music was inspiring
        Sang about justice
             Equality – society without racism
             Rights of people living in poverty
        Sang about love
             Had many children by many different women

The learner can then look at the ideas on the paper, to find what points he wants to emphasize about Bob Marley. He may discover a binding idea: Bob Marley was influential. The tutor's questions lead him to the conclusion that most of the ideas are positive, but he does not approve of Marley's advocating marijuana and having children with many women. The learner then adjusts the main point, or thesis, to: Bob Marley was influential in mostly, but not entirely, positive ways. The essay can now be written, paragraph by paragraph, to develop this idea.

1. Drafting

When a person sets out to write a first draft, the goal is to get ideas on paper, expanding on the ideas produced during planning. Here are some guidelines:

- The first step is to write without worrying about mechanics such as spelling. Stopping to find a word in the dictionary spells death for the ideas the writer is working out on paper.

- Writers can use the ideas from their lists, outlines, or idea maps to start new paragraphs.

- Uncertain spellings can be dealt with any one of these ways:

    Invent a spelling, knowing that spelling can be corrected later.

    Write the first letter and draw a line for the rest of the word.

    Draw a line for the whole word, to be filled in later.

    Ask the tutor or another student to write it on a scrap of paper.

- Learners have an easier time writing if the tutor writes at the same time. If the tutor has trouble getting started, or stops to make changes, that's helpful too in showing the learner that writing can be a struggle for anybody.

Responding to first drafts: After learners and tutors write together, they need to decide whether to share with each other what they wrote. Most writers enjoy the experience of sharing their thoughts and getting a response. Reading the papers aloud to each other, rather than exchanging them to read silently, keeps the focus where it should be: on the ideas expressed, not how the paper looks.

On first hearing, the tutor responds as an interested listener, starting with what he liked and why. The most helpful comments show what came across most strongly and what needs strengthening by referring specifically to the text, such as:

- This letter is very clear. It states exactly what you want.

- I can just imagine the house because you gave such clear details.

- You really made me feel sorry for the little boy.

2. Revising

Revising usually leads to rewriting, which may be a new idea to inexperienced writers. Tutors can reassure learners that most serious writing is the result of much rewriting, because sentences can nearly always be made to sound better. In the writing process, nothing is written in concrete.

Tutors can help with the task of revision by asking learners about their own opinion of the work because self-evaluation is essential for revising. The learner can consider these questions, taking into account why and for whom the piece is being written:

- How do you feel about this piece as a whole?
- Which part do you like best?
- Is there anything you want to change?
- What in particular do you think needs to be worked on?

Since revision is a "re-seeing" of ideas, the tutor can play a key role in helping the writer to "re-see" a piece. Adding, removing, reorganizing or beginning over are all possibilities in the process of revision. Often, beginning writers see no value in what they have written and consider only the fourth possibility, of starting fresh. Tutors should urge learners to build on what they already have produced.

The tutor's questions can also help learners be aware of the future reader, and realize that this reader is not "inside the writer's head." For revising longer pieces, these questions may be helpful:

Content

- Will the reader find this useful or entertaining?
- Are there lively details that catch people's attention?
- Is enough information given?
- Is it original?

Focus

- Is the main point clear?
- Does everything relate in some way to the most important idea?
- Does the title match the text?
- Do the beginning and the end go together?

Organization

- Is there unnecessary repetition?
- Does each paragraph express one main idea?
- Do the sentences in each paragraph relate to the main idea?
- Is the sequence of ideas clear to the reader?

Logic

- Does it make sense?

- Are there enough reasons or explanations for the statements?

- Do the facts lead up to the conclusions?

3. Editing

Editing involves style, thinking about how a piece of writing sounds, including the sentence structure and the choice of words. Since style is a matter of taste and opinion, rather than correctness, final decisions about it belong to the writer.

The tutor should encourage the learner to read the piece aloud during the editing process, so she can hear it for herself. The learner could also ask another person to read or hear the piece and give reactions. Rereading, as well as asking listeners, can help the writer answer these questions:

- Do the words, and how they are used, create the desired impression?

- Will they be understood by the intended audience?

- Are they varied and interesting?

- Do they flow smoothly?

Standard English and Community English: Which version of the English language the writer wants to use is another issue that might come up at the editing stage. English, like most languages, has many versions, based on different speech communities. The differences are of pronunciation, word choice, and grammar, and the communities may be based on region, class, race, or age group. Most people are familiar with these variations, and native speakers have no problem understanding each other.

Most native speakers are familiar with standard English, the version spoken on the radio and written in books, but many prefer to use a community version at home and with their friends. With writing, as with reading and pronouncing words, the user's preferred way of using the language should be acknowledged, understood, and used.

If writers start out writing in the English of their home community, they can decide during the editing phase whether they want to keep it that way or use the more formal dialect of standard English. What they choose will depend on why they are writing and to whom. The English of the community would be right for a letter to a friend, while standard English would probably be appropriate for a report at work or college application. If learners decide that they want to work on standard English for formal communication, practical goals for them would be:

- To hear the difference between community English and standard English.
- To be clear when to use each.
- To be able to use whichever dialect they choose effectively.

The most effective approach to learning standard English forms is to discuss them opportunistically as they come up in the learner's writing. Tutors and learners can also take some time off from writing to explore the patterns of standard English and community dialect. Some frequent differences between community dialect and standard English are with word endings, verb forms and pronouns. For example, learners may need to change these community forms into standard English:

- Add final s on present tense verbs with he, she or it: He seem friendly to me.
- Change past tense verbs: He be working all year round.
- Add s to plural even if number is stated: It wasn't worth five cent.
- Add 's to show ownership with nouns, as in: We went to Mary house.
- Change irregular verb forms: I seen him last night. The car blowed up.
- Change pronoun form: Me and my cousin went to the movies.

Native speakers often know how to make these changes once the difference is pointed out. For learning new information, looking for patterns and creating one's own rules are a good way to learn. This strategy will be described in more detail under "proofreading" in the next pages.

Whatever the learner's goal is concerning standard English, it is important to keep in mind that no native speaker's English is "bad," and that learners should not be made to feel that their dialect is less valuable. Community dialects are rich in ways of expressing things. Who would want to change the expression, "If it ain't broke, don't fix it"? Being able to switch from one language style to another is a valuable life skill. In their efforts to teach children to use standard English, schools have created the impression that other forms of English are wrong or "improper." It is more helpful to think of working on standard English as adding to a person's speech choices, rather than getting rid of imperfections.

4. Proofreading

Proofreading, correcting errors of mechanics, is usually done as the final stage of work on a piece of writing. Some of the most frequent problems center around the following:

- Standard English grammar (see "editing" section above)

    Pronoun use

    Verb tense

    Verb forms

    Adjectives and adverbs

- Punctuation, especially

    Use of apostrophes

    Use of commas

    Capitalization

    Sentences (incomplete, or two run together)

- Spelling
- Omitted words

One way of proofreading, which some people find helpful, is to read the piece backwards, sentence by sentence, starting with the final sentence (read in the normal direction) and working backward to the first. This allows the reader to see the piece with "new eyes" and find things that went unnoticed before. Reading the piece backward removes focus on the sense and ideas of the writing and puts the focus on the correctness of individual sentences.

D. Direct Instruction in Spelling, Punctuation and Grammar

1. Using proofreading to find the learner's needs

Once the proofreading is done, the piece of writing can be considered finished, but the process has probably provided insight into the learner's needs in spelling and punctuation. These can be taught opportunistically during the writing process, or they may be taught after the writing is finished, looking for patterns and rules which will help with not just the one word or sentence, but whole classes of similar ones.

In the long run, the best way to learn to be a better speller is by doing lots of reading to build up a memory of how words look, and by using newly learned words in writing. Repetition in varied contexts is as valuable for spelling as it is for other aspects of reading and writing. But there are direct teaching strategies which help in short run also.

2. Memorizing spelling words

Good spellers have a strong visual memory. They can write a word whose spelling they are unsure of various ways and tell which looks right. Those who learn best from other senses can use those that work for them. Learners might try the following strategies, similar to ways of learning to read sight words, described in Chapter 4, to find out which senses work best for them:

- Visual: Look at the word, then close your eyes and try to see it.
- Auditory, kinesthetic: Say the word aloud (not the letter names) while writing it. The physical act of writing helps those who learn by moving their bodies.
- Tactile, auditory: Trace on a textured surface while saying the word.

These activities can be followed by self-testing and using the word a few times in short lists, then in short sentences.

3. Discovering spelling, grammar and punctuation patterns and rules

As we have said of other learning, patterns and rules for spelling, grammar and punctuation are easily learned and remembered when taught opportunistically based on the need in the student's own writing. Many students benefit from discovering these rules or patterns for themselves, observing and analyzing many examples, rather than being told in advance. The activity of figuring out the rule is like a game. People usually remember and enjoy things in which they have taken an active role.

Suppose, for example that a learner has difficulty spelling words when they take an –ing suffix. Specifically, he misspells stopping and coping. The tutor creates the following word groups:

	stop	stopping
	mop	mopping
	sit	sitting
	run	running
and		
	cope	coping
	have	having
	stare	staring
	smoke	smoking

The learner can observe what happens to the first group of words, that end with a single vowel and a single consonant, when the ending is added, as well as what happens with the second group. He extends his learning by thinking up more examples of each pattern. Running into exceptions or variations is part of the learning process too.

The same approach can be used with punctuation. For example, a student who left out the apostrophe in this phrase:

my mothers house

could be shown a few correctly punctuated examples of a similar pattern:

my mother's house	my husband's niece
my brother's car	our son's friend
his friend's job	a week's pay

and asked, "What's the apostrophe doing there?" Further examples may be needed before the person sees that there is a relation of ownership, or "belonging to" between the owner, which gets the 's, and the thing owned. The tutor may need to help in formulating the rule. Variations, such as what happens for plural "owners" if they end in s, can be taught the same way:

The twin sisters' smiles were identical.

Both dogs' dishes have disappeared.

This strategy of guided analysis, followed by practice, can be used for a number of punctuation facts or other writing conventions, such as using apostrophes for contractions, capitalization of all names, commas with lists, s for plural and ed for past tense. Some of these grammatical forms have been discussed earlier in reference to learning differences between standard English and community English. After a period of direct instruction, the best way to make the new learning stick is to put it to use by doing more writing.

III. SOME QUESTIONS AND ANSWERS ABOUT WRITING

To provide a review of some of the ideas in this chapter, we offer these responses of a tutor coordinator to concerns about writing expressed by tutors and learners:

Q: If the learners do writing at home, isn't it a waste of time to do it during our sessions?

A: The tutor should set aside time during the session because many people find writing very difficult. Writing during the session is easier because the tutor is available to help the students get started and to provide help with such concerns as spelling. By writing with the learners, the tutor also serves as a model. Also, the more writing the better!

Q: What happens if the tutor gives the learners a set amount of time to write, and they hardly write anything?

A: The learners probably feel self-conscious about writing in front of the tutor. The tutor can make it easier for them by writing at the same time. It's much easier to write without someone doing something which looks much easier. As the tutor writes, the learner may feel more comfortable about the writing process from seeing the tutor scratch things out, look out the window, and later hearing that he is not completely satisfied, despite the ability to spell. It might be helpful to provide the learners with something to copy, such as making a grocery list from a newspaper advertisement.

Q: What happens when students say that they have nothing to write, and they don't seem interested in the topics that the tutor suggests?

A: Use the learner's goals. The tutor should encourage the learners to choose the topic, only giving help if needed. Writing can be done in response to reading or as the outgrowth of conversation. Students can keep a list of topics for future writing and add to it frequently. They can brainstorm ideas, or make an idea map or list of questions to be answered.

Q: How can a learner write on her own if she can't spell?

A: Students need to write from the beginning, regardless of spelling ability. They learn to write by writing, and their spelling improves with experience. Any learner can write if she writes down as much of the word as she can, either making up a spelling, trying to get down the first letter, or just leaving a space. After she has written a line or two, she can read it back to the tutor, who writes the words on a separate piece of paper for her before she forgets what she meant to say. She can then copy them into her piece of writing.

Q: What if a student usually hates what he has written and only wants to know how many things he got wrong?

A: The learner may need understanding that a first writing is simply a draft, and can be changed or added to later. The student can look at the tutor's own messy, crossed-out drafts that he has been doing during the sessions and realize that writers are not always happy with the results of their efforts.

Learners need to realize that seeing the good points in their own writing helps them to grow as writers, while belittling themselves interferes with learning. Rather than thinking of "number wrong," they should decide what they need help with. They are in charge of their own learning.

IV. CONCLUSION

Writing is an extremely valuable learning activity on many levels. It is important to all of us because it is a way of sorting out our ideas and a way of making ourselves heard by near and distant audiences. Writing can begin right away, regardless of the student's ability. Doing ample reading will improve writing, and doing ample writing will improve reading. We encourage tutors and learners to put time and energy into this enriching experience.

Chapter 6

Working With Computers

Computers are so much a part of life today that adult literacy learners usually welcome the chance to learn about using them. Like other machines in our lives, from television to automobiles, people like to understand how they work, how to use them, and how to avoid the risks they pose.

This chapter will suggest ways that tutors and learners can gain experience in using them for writing, gathering information, and learning. What to focus on depends on the learner's goals. For most people, having some understanding of how a computer works helps them to use it with confidence.

Tutors do not have to be experts in computers to use them with a learner. Computer learning is a great equalizer, with tutors and learners learning about them together. Sometimes the learner is the one who figures out why a computer is not working as expected.

I. COMPUTERS AND THE ADULT LEARNER

Adult literacy learners, like everybody else, have had frustrating experiences with computers, if not while trying to use them, then with hearing office workers who have lost some important information say, "Oh, the computer made a mistake," as though the computer had a mind of its own.

Adult literacy learners who have never used a computer probably have mixed feelings about them. They may feel intimidated by them because they have heard how difficult, expensive, or even dangerous, they are. They might be afraid of damaging it or of being unable to learn to use it.

On the other hand, they may feel a strong need to learn to use computers. They may fear that if they don't learn to use computers, their children and friends will look down on them. They see them used all around them, by children in school from the early grades on, and in every occupation from retail clerks to delivery drivers to farmers. They may also have hopes that if they can learn to use computers they will be better qualified for a job or able to help their children in school.

II. WORKING TOGETHER WITH COMPUTERS

A. What to Study

What a learner does with a computer depends on her goals, but whatever they might be the computer can provide reading material through the Internet and a tool for writing through word processing. In addition, people who want to do office work might need to use computers for:

- word processing
- spreadsheets and databases
- making calculations
- designing presentations
- e-mail
- Internet searches

All these tasks require being able to type, use a mouse or touchpad, and handle files.

1. Learning about computers

Having a basic understanding of what makes a computer work takes some of the mystery out of it and makes it easier to get started.

2. Word processing

One of the best uses of a computer in a tutoring session is word processing because it makes writing of any kind easier and better.

Word processing improves people's writing in several ways:

- It allows the writer to produce a clean, clear, copy. Even if a printer is not available at the site, work can be saved on a disc and printed elsewhere.
- Once a person learns to type, writing is faster and more comfortable.
- Because words can be moved or removed, learners will do more revising, thereby producing better work.

Since most computers come with a word processing application, it is easy for learners and tutors to get started.

3. Instructional programs

Besides programs for learning word processing, there are computer programs to teach nearly everything a learner might want, from vocabulary to mathematics to resumé writing.

One of the advantages a computer learning program has over a textbook or exercise practice book is its ability to give immediate correction, often with explanation. Another advantage is that correction coming from a computer often feels less critical than the most carefully worded comments coming from a human. A third advantage is that a learner at a keyboard is more likely to feel in charge of his own learning.

There is a great deal of software for learning available on the Internet, but its quality is uneven. The tutor can always try programs herself, though this can be time-consuming. Staff and other tutors can probably recommend material. Each learning program needs to be evaluated for relevance to the learner's goals, ease of use, and instructional value. Software that is created for children is often inappropriate for adults, as programs with giggles, whistles, and goofy characters are likely to irritate an adult learner.

Typing: Programs to teach touch typing are helpful for people starting to use the computer, since the computer is run by typing, and the keyboard to be learned is already at the learner's fingertips. Knowing how to type makes using the computer easier and is a useful skill for any writing task.

Numeracy: Most computers have software calculators and spreadsheet programs for learning a range of mathematical and accounting tasks. These could be used to do some of the activities described in Chapter 7.

Information technology: Learners who already know something about computers might want to learn other information technology skills, such as working with databases and making presentations. Since these can get complicated, the tutor would need to be familiar with the material.

4. Internet searching

Guided by the learner's goals and interests, learners and tutors can use Internet search engines such as Google or Yahoo! to find reading material on any topic. To start a search with Google, for example, you type http://www.google.com. The problem is usually one of finding too many, rather than too few sites.

Materials available include:

- pieces of literature: stories, poems, plays
- newspapers and magazines from all over the world
- dictionaries
- encyclopedias
- GED practice exams

While reading long selections on a computer screen is not a good use of tutoring time – why not get the book? – poems, or parts of stories and plays could be read and printed for repeated reading.

Since there are web sites that will read aloud to the learner, a learner who is not ready to read the newspaper independently could listen to the computer read aloud as the learner followed. This application requires Internet access and a speaker connected to the computer.

5. E-mail

With Internet access, it is possible to get a free e-mail account and use it to write and receive e-mail messages. Using e-mail provides an opportunity for writing and knowing how to use e-mail is a component of computer job readiness. Typing "free e-mail" on a search engine such as Google will give information on such accounts, which are paid for by the advertisements they sell rather than the users.

B. How to Do It

1. Learning about computers

Once the learner's goals for computer learning have been established, the tutor can begin by sharing what she knows about the basics. This includes connecting all necessary cables, turning the computer on, and using a keyboard and mouse or other pointing device.

It also includes giving the learner an idea, in everyday terms, of what a computer is and how it works. The following information provides a useful base for starting to work with computers:

a) Knowing the difference between hardware and software

- Hardware is the equipment: what you can see and touch.
- Software is the electronically recorded set of instructions that makes the computer do its work.

b) Names for hardware

- The central processing unit (CPU) with the circuit board on which all the electronic connections are made.
- The monitor, with the screen.
- The keyboard and the mouse.
- The printer.
- Discs or other means of storing information for safety and for transferring to other computers.

c) Description

- A computer stores, manages and retrieves information.

- The information is handled by electrically coded instructions: the software

- The computer connects to telephone lines or cable TV lines for e-mail and the Internet.

- The computer works by sets of electric connections clicking on and off at extremely high speeds.

- Everything a computer does could be done by human brains, but the computer can hold more information, and it does its work much, much, faster.

- A computer doesn't "think" on its own; it only sorts and calculates what a programmer has programmed it to do.

Learners may enjoy realizing that the people who say, "The computer made a mistake," aren't telling it quite right. A human being gave the wrong orders or the wrong information somewhere along the line.

d) First steps

- If the computer isn't already set up, the learner can watch and learn as the tutor connects the appropriate cables and turns it on.

- The tutor shows how to locate and open the desired program, for example a program for learning how to do word processing or typing.

- The learner sits at the keyboard and reads the screen, ready to begin typing and moving and clicking the mouse, with the tutor's guidance.

2. Word processing

Learners may want to use a touch typing program to learn to type quickly without looking at the keys, or they may be happy to "hunt and peck," which can be done quickly with practice.

The learner and tutor have the choice of using a program to learn word processing or having the tutor explain and demonstrate from her own knowledge. If they decide not to use a learning program, the tutor could demonstrate tasks in the following order:

- Opening a new word processing document by pointing and clicking the mouse.
- Moving the cursor to the desired spot for writing.
- Typing a few lines, using the space bar and "enter."
- Highlighting and deleting.
- Moving text by copying, cutting, pasting and dragging.
- Naming and saving a document.
- Printing or transferring to a disc to print elsewhere.
- Using a spell checking program to find typing or spelling errors.

> Learners will find that a spell check does not tell them how to spell the word they want, it just gives them some correctly spelled words to choose from.

Seeing their work in print for the first time is an exciting experience for most learners.

Any of the writing activities described in Chapter 5, "Writing," can be done on a word processor once the student becomes comfortable with the process. Doing one of these writing projects on a computer combines a wide range of activities, skills, and interests. For example, if a learner writes a letter to the editor about a news article he just read, he will combine reading, writing and computer skills.

Once learners get used to word processing, they might want to learn to do more elaborate things, from multiple styles and colors of type, to adding clip art pictures or digital photographs.

3. Instructional programs

The tutor does not have to be an expert in the topic of an instructional program, though it helps to know something about it. What the tutor has to know is how to start and operate the instructional software. It is a good idea to try a program out in advance to make sure it works as described, so that the learner can use it without frustration.

When using instructional software

- The learner should feel free to stop when fatigued. Fifteen minutes might be enough for a person just getting started.
- The tutor and learner can talk beforehand about how much help the learner wants in reading the screen, deciding on what to do, and typing.

4. Internet searches

The tutor can explain how to open up the Internet, with the necessary http://www, and demonstrate how a search engine makes searching more efficient by not requiring a particular web site, just key words, with or without quotation marks.

The learner can practice using a search engine such as Google by typing in key words relating to a topic she would like to know more about. If thousands of entries come up because the request was too broad, the tutor can guide the learner into a narrower topic by using more than one key word. Stories, plays, or poems can be found by typing a title, lines from a poem in quotation marks, or the author's full name.

Once a file has been opened, the learner can:

- Read it on the screen, which can be hard on the eyes and easy to forget.

- Print the whole document, which can use up too much time and paper.

- Copy a selection off the screen into a word processing program to print for later reading.

5. E-mail

Learners with Internet access can get experience writing for a real audience while learning about e-mail. They can start by collecting e-mail addresses of friends, including the tutor, then write and send messages.

The tutor can help the learner with these steps:

- finding a free e-mail address
- opening the application
- addressing the letter and giving it a "subject"
- giving the usual greeting and closing
- writing the message
- sending the message
- receiving mail

Spam and other advertising: The tutor should also show the learner how to close or delete unsolicited "spam" e-mail and pop-up advertisements, many of which are sexually offensive.

The tutor should remind the learner that false advertising schemes are just as likely on the Internet as on television or over the telephone. Talking about spam will add to the learner's consumer awareness.

III. SOME QUESTIONS AND ANSWERS ABOUT USING COMPUTERS

These questions from tutors and learners, and the answers given by coordinators, supplement or review some of the important ideas in this chapter.

Q: Where will I begin?

A: Most learners and tutors like to spend some time exploring. There are programs that introduce the keyboard and teach typing skills. Some people prefer to get started by playing some of the games that give keyboard experience without the pressure of learning anything else. Others might prefer diving right into lessons.

Q: What if I break it?

A: You won't.

Q: I'm not ready yet.

A: Most learners who have come to the computer sites have felt good about their experiences. One student said, "There are a lot of people out there who are afraid of computers. We just come in and give them a try and it works." There are materials at a variety of levels and, as we said before, with the right methods, more difficult material can be used with a basic level learner. Much of the software allows for putting in one's own material. This works especially well with language experience stories.

If tutors do not feel ready, they can:

- Come alone until they are comfortable coming with the learner. They can find people to help and materials which explain the computers and the software.
- Ask agency staff for training or additional assistance.
- Suggest that the learners go alone to the computer center, and work with staff there.
- Tutors should not hold learners back and should not worry about what the learners will think if the tutor has any difficulty. Learning together is an excellent opportunity for working together as partners.

IV. CONCLUSION

A computer is a piece of equipment for reading, writing, and calculating. Learners can appreciate the ease that word processing brings to writing, use the "information highway" of the Internet for an electronic "visit to the library," and enjoy taking advantage of one of today's electronic conveniences.

Chapter 7

Numeracy

L earners who come to adult literacy programs often want to develop their ability to work with numbers as well as their reading and writing. They realize that they need skills in math to accomplish their goals. They need it for a variety of purposes, including handling money, measuring things, and reading numerical information with understanding. They also know that increased math proficiency will help them to make decisions and judgments involving the use of numbers.

Adult learners benefit by a balanced approach to math learning. As with reading and writing, learners are most successful when they plan their programs according to how they will use numbers in their lives. We offer a guide to the ways tutors and learners can draw on adult learners' experiences to help them learn mathematics.

I. WHAT IS NUMERACY?

Literacy with numbers: Numeracy, the ability to use numbers comfortably in daily life, is one aspect of literacy. It includes, but is not limited to, being able to do calculations. A numerate person has the following abilities:

- Understands how the number system works, and so is able to estimate and choose the right procedures before doing any calculations.

- Reads the newspaper and understands the meanings of the numbers, measures, calculations, charts and tables presented, just as a literate person is able to understand the meanings of words.

- Uses mathematics to accomplish the tasks of day-to-day life.

Although "numeracy" has a broader meaning than knowledge of mathematical principles, we find the terms "math" and "numeracy" close enough in meaning to use them interchangeably in this handbook.

Examples of using numeracy to read the news: The newspaper *USA Today* provides an example of how reading includes understanding numbers. In any section, whether the front page, "Sports," "Money," or "Life," the reader will find numerically presented information, including charts and graphs related to news, weather, finance, advertisements, box scores in the sports section, and headlines. A good reader will answer questions using numbers while thinking about many items, as in the following:

- The big weather map: Estimating the temperature in her area by its color on the map: How will the temperature tomorrow affect how she will dress or what she will do?

- A car rental ad offering a car for $39.99/day or $199.99/week: Does it make sense to rent by the week? Does the company offer a good price in general? Why don't they just charge the extra penny and say $40 and $200? If her car broke down today, could she fit this car rental into her budget? Or, does public transportation make more sense?

A person who can handle these questions is numerate, able to bring meaning to the numbers by applying his knowledge and experience.

Making meaning: As with reading and writing, numeracy involves making meaning. Doing math with understanding is as important as reading with comprehension or writing to express meaningful ideas. In all three cases, learning is most successful when it uses the learners' existing knowledge and experience and is applied to their own needs.

Math has vocabulary and symbols of its own which must be learned. A numerate person must be able to translate real-life problems into mathematical terms, such as knowing how much money to withdraw from an ATM. Working with number problems in advance, learning the symbols, the terms and the procedures prepares people for these problems.

The greatest danger in learning and teaching math is learning certain procedures on paper, such as going through the correct steps for adding fractions with different denominators, without understanding the reason for these procedures. If people master math procedures and do well on a test without understanding what they are doing, their math learning will be of little use in daily life.

II. NUMERACY AND THE ADULT LEARNER

Math is essential, yet undervalued in our society. We need it in nearly everything we do to meet basic needs such as these:

- Managing our money, both earning it and spending it.
- Understanding trends and statistics in the news.
- Making informed choices in elections and major decisions such as jobs, health care or where to live.
- Engaging in occupations and hobbies that build things, both in designing and constructing them.

Yet, many people say they "can't do math" and avoid numbers whenever they can. Their willingness to give up on math suggests that they see math as very difficult and not very important. Yet, they do so to their own loss, for in avoiding numbers they limit their chances to gain competence in many activities.

A. Negative Feelings About Math

Tutors will probably find that teaching numeracy as a real life activity is as interesting and as much fun as teaching reading and writing. Learners may need to overcome some negative feelings about math, as with reading and writing, before they can enjoy learning it.

Humiliation: Adult learners may have negative feelings about math because of unpleasant memories of math in school, where they were made to feel stupid because they did not learn as fast or remember as well as other learners.

Blind memorization: Perhaps they were taught procedures, such as borrowing for subtraction or reducing fractions to their lowest terms, with no opportunity to understand the reasons for them. When they did not understand a topic, they had no choice but to learn by memorizing procedures, and when their memories failed them, they had no basis for estimating. Adults who see math as memorization and who think that they have poor memories may be convinced that they can never do math.

Drudgery: Another problem for adult learners is that they may have experienced math instruction which emphasized accuracy and repetitious practice, such as adding long columns of five-digit numbers or pages of long division. Because they did not experience math as a thinking, problem-solving process, they saw math study as drudgery, rather than exploration.

These combined issues have had a serious impact on many adult learners. Feelings of personal inadequacy and a distaste for numbers are challenges the tutors and students may need to meet.

B. How Can These Negative Feelings Be Overcome?:

First, tutors and learners can discuss some common myths surrounding mathematics:

The Myth: People are either born with math ability or they will never have it.
The Truth: Everyone can learn math, and improvement comes with practice. People who are good at math now worked to gain that ability; it didn't just come to them.

The Myth: Being good at math means being good at calculating.
The Truth: Understanding math means understanding the ideas behind the math. In order for the math to be useful, one has to know how to look at a real-life need and apply a process to address it. The ability and speed with which one calculates improves with practice.

The Myth: Women can't do math as well as men.
The Truth: This myth has absolutely no biological basis. There is a long list of women who have been and continue to be pioneers in the field of mathematics. Some women have had limited achievement in math because they were brought up believing this stereotype.

Adults' strengths for learning math: When a learner is in the midst of an episode of math anxiety, saying: "I can't do math" or "I'm no good at numbers," it helps to remind him of the numeracy skills he uses with quantities and amounts in everyday life.

- If the learner can find an address, he must have a fairly good concept of number sequences.

- Learners use numbers when they think about getting places on time, shopping, calendars, phone numbers, I.D. numbers, and maps.

- Some learners are skilled at using a calculator.

- Most adults can tell time, whether digital or on a clock face, and virtually all learners know that half an hour is thirty minutes and an hour is sixty minutes.

- Most adult learners are skilled at handling money in daily life, counting their change, reading decimal fractions in prices with dollars and cents, planning money for bus fares or grocery shopping, and calculating what is owed them for work at an hourly rate. Learners who think they are incompetent in math may not think of their use of money as "real" math, but their knowledge of money can be used with more abstract problems.

What learners already know can be used as a springboard for further work with numbers. For example, learners can gain a deeper understanding of fractions, including percents and decimals, by building on what they know about a half dollar:

50 cents is half a dollar.

50 cents out of one hundred cents in a dollar is half a dollar.

50 cents can be written as .50.

Furthermore, 50% means 50 out of 100.

Therefore, 50% is equal to 1/2.

"Cents" is a root meaning 100.

Digits two places to the right of a decimal represent hundredths.

III. WORKING TOGETHER ON MATHEMATICS

A. What to Do

As with other aspects of literacy, learner goals should determine what methods and materials are used for studying math. Tutors and learners can look over the math items in the Goals Checklist described in Chapter 2, and later go back to the checklist as learners accomplish each goal.

1. Real world number situations

Solving problems using real world number situations has several advantages.

- It shows learners how math relates to their lives.
- It shows them how they are already using math.
- It helps the learner become self-reliant in achieving number goals.
- It gives an understanding of how the number system works and what operations do.
- It provides the opportunity for concepts to be learned through concrete examples.
- It develops general proficiency with numbers.
- It provides practice for learners whose goal is to pass the General Education Development test, as that test consists entirely of problems simulating real-life situations.

The following activities, involving measurement of time, money, and other entities, suggest ways learners and tutors might begin to work with the numbers in their lives.

a) Time

Learners might want to work with dates and time of day. Here are some suggestions for work in this area:

Reading a calendar: A calendar can be used to discuss the following questions:

- What do the numbers on the calendar represent?

- How many columns are on the calendar, and which days of the week do they represent?

- Does a calendar week start with Sunday or Monday? Is the English system different from the Spanish one?

Answering these questions can lead to a look at varying number systems, such as seven for the week, twelve for the year, and a range from 28 to 31 for the months.

Writing dates: Learners might want to learn both ways of writing dates. Here is one approach:

Tutor says or writes:	*Learner writes:*
May 1, 1995	5/1/95
January 23, 2001	_____
March 11, 2004	_____

Learners and tutors can discuss where these might be used. How they write the dates would depend on their goals, whether they want to date a quick note for themselves, a check, or a formal letter.

Writing clock time: Learners can learn how to write down the time of day. They could try these for practice:

Tutor says:	*Learner writes:*
(I got up at) seven thirty in the morning.	7:30 a.m.
(The appointment is for) ten o'clock.	_____
(Be home by) half past six tonight.	_____
(I arrived at) five after seven in the morning.	_____

(I punched in at) eight fifty-three. _____

A quarter of six (is too late). _____

(The phone rang at) one fifteen in the morning. _____

(We expect to go at) four thirty in the afternoon. _____

Calculating hours: Learners may need to learn to calculate hours for such purposes as time sheets at work. This requires a specialized way of counting. Ordinary adding and subtracting do not work, because a clock is based on a system of two sets of 12 to make up the total of 24 hours. Looking at the face of a clock, learners can practice counting the hours before twelve o'clock, and adding them to the hours after twelve.

Learners can do these:

9:00 A.M. - 3:00 P.M. _____ hours

10:30 A.M. - 6:00 P.M. _____ hours

7:30 P.M. - 2:15 A.M. _____ hours

A.M. and P.M. Learners might be interested to learn the roots of A.M. and P.M., ante and post, for general knowledge as well as to help remember which is before and which is after noon, or the meridian.

Military time: Some people want to learn to read military time, which is used for schedules in many countries. It is easier to calculate because it is based on 24 hours, but harder to read because the afternoon and evening hours do not match our clock faces. It begins with 00:01 for one minute after midnight, proceeds through the morning hours to 12:59, then goes to 13:00 (for 1:00 P.M.) and continues to 24:00 for midnight.

b) Money

Learners may want to start using banks and become more involved in managing their household finances. Working with money requires knowledge of arithmetic. In order to count their change and calculate their expenses, learners must be skilled in subtraction and addition, and in order to calculate sales, tips and taxes, they need to understand the relationship between fractions, decimals and percents.

Managing a checking account:
Learners may want to learn how to use a checkbook. This task is a good example of a situation combining reading, writing and math. Learners can work on all three aspects of the task by:

- Making a chart of the spelling of number words to keep in their wallets for reference.

- Filling in photocopies of blank checks.

- Filling in and subtracting and/or adding entries on the stubs.

- Balancing the monthly statement against the checks and the stubs.

Bills: Tax forms and bills of all kinds also combine reading, writing and math. If learners and tutors feel comfortable doing so, they can work on actual bills together. The complexity of the telephone bill, for example, makes it a challenge for many people. Tutors and learners can:

- Read the document, using echo reading or the tutor reading aloud to the learner, if necessary.

- Discuss any part that is unclear, for instance, finding where the amount due is indicated.

- Explore consumer issues by reading information about late payment charges or finance charges.

- Calculate yearly finance charges, first writing monthly percents as decimals before multiplying, then multiplying the answers by 12 months.

c) Measuring

The tutor or the learner can bring to the session a tape measure, a yardstick or a ruler, and learners will gain the benefit of learning and using mathematical concepts in concrete situations. Measurement while doing all kinds of projects, from cooking to home maintenance, offers the opportunity for learning the following concepts and procedures:

- For sewing, painting or carpentry, learning would include how to find the perimeter and area of squares and rectangles.

- Practice in measuring things will help the learners make the connection between geometry and arithmetic. They will literally see what a geometric formula represents.

- Learners can practice addition and multiplication and work with formulas.

- Learners can gain experience using measuring tape, rulers and yardsticks, with the tutor guiding as they measure windows, rugs, floors, tables, books and anything else within reach.

- Reading fractions of inches on a tape can lead to working on comprehension of fractions, as described later in this chapter.

Finding perimeters: To find the distance around something, with guidance from the tutor, learners can measure or draw and label, then calculate the length of:

- The baseboard around the room.
- The frame around a picture.
- The fringes around a scarf or a rug.

Learners can see for themselves that adding the length and the width and doubling the result is the easiest way to find the perimeter of these rectangles.

Learning formulas: When they see a perimeter, they can also see that the formula is a shorthand statement, using the initial of the dimension and certain conventions, such as parentheses for multiplication. These are the usual formulas for different types of four-sided figures:

perimeter of a rectangle: $P = 2 (L + W)$

perimeter of a square: $P = 4 S$

perimeter of an irregular quadrilateral: $P = L1 + L2 + L3 + L4$

Learners can also see relations between operations with these examples:

- With a rectangle, 2 (L + W), using multiplication, is more compactly written and easier to calculate than this way of writing the same information: L + L + W + W.

- For the perimeter of a square, 4S is more compact and easier to calculate than S+S+S+S.

Finding areas: The tutor and learners can measure or draw sketches, then find:

- The area of the room they are in.
- How much wrapping paper would cover a package.
- The surface of the table.
- How many one-foot tiles might cover a kitchen floor.

Learners can see by drawing in the square feet of a 4 by 3 foot space how multiplication will give them the answer they need.

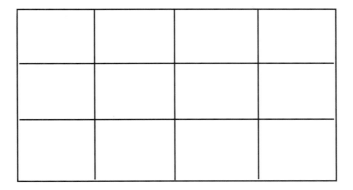

As with perimeter, they can see how the formulas for the areas of a rectangle and a square express the idea of multiplying the sides:

area of a rectangle: $A = LW$

area of a square: $A = S2$

Exponents: The formula for the area of a square provides an opportunity for the learner to find out about the concept of a number multiplied once by itself, why it is called a square, and how it is written. How it is written could also lead to a discussion of the use of exponents in general: how a number can be written as multiplied by itself any number of times.

$5 \times 5 \times 5 \times 5 \times 5 \times 5$

can be written: 5^6 and referred to as "five to the sixth power."

Using numbers in projects: The measuring needed for any project the learner wants to work on provides an excellent way of working on math. For example, a learner who had in mind a house maintenance project could begin with making estimates, then following with measurements and calculations. With guidance from the tutor, the learner could estimate and calculate the quantity and cost of materials and the time needed, by doing the following:

- Measuring the rooms, in inches as well as feet, to find the area.
- Calculating the number of gallons of paint needed for that area.
- Calculating the cost of the paint.
- Adding the cost of such materials as patching plaster, sandpaper, and tools.
- Adding a little extra so as not to run out of materials.
- Adding up the probable hours for each task to estimate how long the project should take.

The math calculations include multiplication, addition, and division. After talking through the problem and deciding which operation to use, the learner could use a calculator. He can be reminded that many people use a calculator for tedious and exacting tasks such as balancing a checkbook or to check up on the work they did by hand.

B. Materials To Use

1. Numbers in written materials

As we said when defining "numeracy," reading, writing, and using numbers often are used together in the world, especially in newspapers and magazines. Here are some suggestions for using them with learners:

Newspapers and magazines: Learners or tutors might work with the following:

- Advertisements, to plan shopping for groceries, clothes, gifts, household items, a car or a new house or apartment.

- Cost of items: Amount saved when items are on sale and comparison of similar items.

- News stories with numbers expressed in percents, fractions, or decimals.

- News stories with large statistics, such as the number of cigarette smokers or homicide deaths for different parts of the country.

- Graphs, such as pie charts, telling how government money is allocated or bar graphs to compare numbers of persons executed.

  Graphs are discussed in more detail later in this chapter.

Consumer texts: Learners can bring in any catalogues and store coupons that interest them. They can calculate the total cost of a list of items, and how much is saved by using coupons instead of paying the regular price. Catalogues can be studied for the total cost of items combined with shipping and taxes.

2. Math workbooks

Math workbooks present a structured approach to math. The workbooks which have answers in the back are by far the most useful, as they allow learners to catch their own mistakes at home and develop the habit of independent learning. While the tutor is the best source of explanations, workbooks can be used as a reminder of what was done in the sessions. A well-written workbook provides these benefits:

- Practice in class in using new concepts immediately.
- Opportunity for independent practice and self-checking at home.

After learners try problems, they can look up the answers, and look back at their work to see if any error they made was the result of carelessness or of not understanding something.

- Learners can reread the explanation in the book at home if they forget what was said in the session.
- Workbooks' structured approach helps learners find particular topics.
- Learners whose goal is passing the GED or getting into more advanced education or training programs will find workbooks helpful for developing more advanced knowledge, such as finding square roots, calculating what percent one number is of another, or deriving the radius of a circle from its circumference.

The chief drawback of workbooks is that they may not be focused on any particular learner's needs and interests. They are best used in combination with the real-world materials that are suggested by the learner's goals. One tutor has said she and her learners use a workbook the way she uses a cookbook, using whatever sections suit her purpose and making changes and additions based on her own experience.

C. Tutoring Strategies

Learners and tutors need to do learning activities which provide a good understanding of numbers. As with other learning, number-related activities are best learned when modeled by someone else, then done by the learner with gradually decreasing support. Learners need to understand the concept, apply it, get monitoring from someone else, and connect the new concepts with everyday life.

In this section we give examples to describe steps for teaching math procedures, followed by guidelines for two teaching/learning strategies that are particularly helpful in numeracy study:

- Estimating: We have already mentioned the importance of estimating for written math problems just as the learners do mental estimates of time, money, and other quantities in their daily lives.

- Hands-on experience: Learners benefit from counting, cutting up, or arranging objects as they work with math concepts such as fractions or regrouping.

1. Steps for working on math together

Successful math learning usually begins with the learner observing someone do a number task, then trying it, with assistance and feedback, and repeating it, with decreasing assistance. In a small group working on math, the stages might take this form:

a) Observing as the tutor models the task

The learners watch while the tutor demonstrates and explains how to write up and solve a problem involving the addition of whole numbers and decimal fractions:

```
  5.00
  1.50
+  .25
  6.75
```

b) Copying the tutor

The learners first copy the model by telling the tutor how to set up a similar problem:

- The tutor says, "How should I write it to add 3, 2.65, and 5.32?"

- The tutor writes up and solves the problem when the right instructions are given, explaining why incorrect suggestions will not work.

- The tutor repeats the process with more complex variations, such as, "How would we add .125 and 17.50 and .03?"

c) Doing the task with others, giving and getting help

When a group of learners are working with one tutor, they can work independently some of the time, helping each other, in twos or threes, with similar problems.

d) Doing the task independently

In class, and later at home, learners work alone on more problems given by the tutor. They receive feedback from either the tutor, other learners, or an answer key. Finally, they demonstrate their knowledge of the new concepts and procedures by making up similar problems and explaining their solution to other learners.

Tutors and learners can work out variations of this sequence according to the complexity of the task and the size and ability of the group.

2. Estimating

Why is estimating important? The ability to estimate is essential for just about any situation involving numbers. Estimates help people plan, and they serve as a check against mistakes. In everyday life, most people estimate more often than they make exact calculations. People estimate when counting their change, getting to places on time, looking over a bill in a restaurant, or figuring out the cost of groceries before they get in the checkout line. Learners should be encouraged to get in the habit of estimating their answers before completing any problem.

These are the benefits:

- Learners can think about the meaning of what they are doing before using memorized procedures.
- They can focus on the important aspects of a problem before getting into the details of calculation.
- They can catch their own mistakes, especially if a small error in computation, pressing the wrong button on the calculator, or doing the wrong operation, produced a ridiculous answer.
- Estimating builds learners' self-reliance.
- For tutors, having the learners estimate before calculating precisely reveals how well they understand a math procedure.

How can estimating be learned? Estimating requires looking at place value which is discussed later in this chapter. In explaining about estimating, the tutor can point out that we round off numbers to whatever is convenient: tens, hundreds or thousands. We often round off to dollars by removing the hundredths, or cents.

The tutor can demonstrate the advantage of rounding off to the nearest ten in the following problem:

$$\begin{array}{r} 183 \\ -27 \\ \hline \end{array}$$

Instead of working with single digits, and taking time for the regrouping (borrowing) process, a learner can look at the problem as a whole, rounding off both numbers to the nearest ten in this way:

$$\begin{array}{r} 180 \\ -\ 30 \\ \hline \end{array}$$

The learner can further round off by subtracting 3 from 18, and conclude that about 180 minus about 30 is about 150. A learner who estimates an answer this way, before working it out, will gain a better understanding of regrouping for subtraction.

3. Using hands-on experience to teach concepts

Why is handling objects helpful? Concepts are often learned best when they are illustrated with objects learners can handle or expressed in terms learners can visualize because several senses are involved in addition to abstract thinking. Time spent handling and arranging objects to illustrate the mathematical operations can dramatically increase learners' understanding of math, thereby building self-confidence.

What can learners use? Common household objects can be used: anything that can be carried in large quantities, such as toothpicks, buttons, beans, or paper clips.

Learners may need some demonstration of how to manipulate the objects, since the learners may not be used to working in math this way. For multiplication and division, they could take 12 beans and arrange them in rows, showing that in one direction they form three rows of four beans each, and in the other, four rows of three. They are illustrating that:

$$4 + 4 + 4 = 12 \qquad \text{or} \qquad 3 \times 4 = 12$$
$$3 + 3 + 3 + 3 = 12 \qquad \text{or} \qquad 4 \times 3 = 12$$

Money is something that everybody understands. Pennies, dimes and dollar bills can be helpful for learning place value as well as decimals and fractions. Lining up one penny, one dime and one dollar bill demonstrates the place for the digits representing ones, tens and hundreds. The tutor can explain regrouping (borrowing) as changing a dime from the tens place into ten pennies, so as to be able to subtract pennies from pennies.

D. Basic Numeracy Topics

In this section, we focus on four topics which are essential for understanding and manipulating numbers. First, we discuss place value, because learners need to fully understand our system of place value to read large numbers, to understand decimals, and to do calculations. Next, we present strategies for teaching fractions, decimals and percents so learners can comprehend and manipulate numbers that represent parts of a whole. Third, we focus on graphs, which are important for reading technical information. Finally, we describe how mastering number facts of addition, subtraction, multiplication, and division can be combined with other math learning.

1. Understanding place value

Understanding place value is key to understanding, comparing, and manipulating numbers. A dieter watching calories may look at a calorie list and discover that a glass of grapefruit juice has 95 calories, while a chocolate shake has 480. If that person did not understand the function of zero in establishing place value, he might assume that the juice has more calories, because it starts with a larger number.

Place value is also important when doing math operations. For instance, many learners can complete this problem correctly by regrouping (borrowing):

$$\begin{array}{r} 83 \\ - \ 39 \\ \hline 44 \end{array}$$

but do not realize that one of the tens in 83 is regrouped ("borrowed") from its 8 tens, and is not just "a one" regrouped (borrowed) from "the eight." They need to understand that one of the tens is regrouped as ten ones and added to the three ones.

Learners with a limited understanding of place value will frequently misalign columns when doing multi-digit addition or subtraction problems. This is especially true when working with decimals.

Here are two ways to demonstrate place value:

Dots can represent groups of tens and ones for three numbers:

Tens	Ones	
*********	***	
*********		= 2 tens + 3 ones = 23
*********	****	
*********		= 2 tens + 4 ones = 24
*********	*****	
*********		= 2 tens + 5 ones = 25

A three-place number may be regrouped as a sum of hundreds, tens and ones:

625
600 + 20 + 5
6 x 100 + 2 x 10 + 5 x 1
6 x 10 x 10 + 2 x 10 + 5 x 1

Because of adults' experience with it, money is an excellent real life item to use when working with place value, using pennies, dimes, and dollars. Tutors and learners can use pocket change for small quantities, while they can construct mock money or use the money from games such as Monopoly for larger quantities.

Understanding large numbers:

Understanding the world that we live in sometimes requires us to think about the numbers that are beyond our day-to-day experience. For example, a newspaper might refer to a U.S. population of nearly 300 million people (292,900,592 and counting, as of this writing) or a national debt of nearly $7 trillion ($6,904,718,859,459.11, as revealed by an Internet search, as of this writing).

Here is one way to imagine the terms million, billion, and trillion:

1 million seconds equals about 12 days (a nice amount of time for vacation).

1 billion seconds equals about 32 years (about the age of some learners).

1 trillion seconds equals about 32,000 years (longer than the recorded history of humanity).

While million, billion, and trillion are all large numbers, one can see from the above illustration how far apart they are from one another.

Place value for reading large numbers: Learners who do not understand place value usually have trouble reading numbers larger than a thousand. The tutor can help them understand the concept by making a place value chart like the one that follows which describes the number 763,574,291. The tutor can draw or refer to the chart, explaining that it accounts for numbers up to one million, and that billions, trillions, and so forth are likewise arranged and read in groups of three. The tutor can demonstrate, and learners can practice:

- Reading numbers in the chart format, from left to right.
- Naming each group of three within each box as millions, thousands, and ones.

After working with the chart, learners can try reading numbers written in the conventional format, with commas marking groups of three. They should be reminded that although numbers are read from left to right, as in reading sentences, the commas in large numbers are placed by threes, from right to left.

Place Value Chart for Reading Large Numbers

Read:

Seven hundred
sixty-three million

M
I
L
L
I
O
N

763

Read:

five hundred
seventy-four
thousand

T
H
O
U
S
A
N
D

574

Read:

two hundred
thirty-six
(We don't say "ones.")

O
N
E
S

236

Try reading this number:

864,952,437

M
I
L
L
I
O
N

864

T
H
O
U
S
A
N
D

952

O
N
E
S

437

Now try reading these:

379, 452, 003

125, 683, 799

306, 498, 216

Students might want to know about another useful way of writing large numbers: scientific notation. Scientists use exponents of 10. One hundred is two tens multiplied together.

$100 = 10 \times 10 = 10^2$

Instead of writing one million with six zeroes, they write it as an exponent of ten, or ten multiplied together six times, that is:

$1,000,000 = 10 \times 10 \times 10 \times 10 \times 10 \times 10 = 10^6$

The three additional zeroes of one billion increase the exponent:

$1,000,000,000 = 10^9$

Learning exponents while studying large numbers is an example of opportunistic learning, in which a topic is learned as a natural expansion of something else that is being studied.

2. Fractions, decimals, and percents

These are ways of expressing parts of a whole, usually of values less than one. A part can be expressed in all three ways. A dime, for example, can be spoken of as 1/10, .1, or 10% of a dollar. People tend to favor decimals for written communication and detailed statistical analysis, while speakers often favor fractions and percents. A conversion table for percents, fractions, and decimals may be found in Appendix 3.

Fractions: It is helpful to teach fractions with concrete aids, so that learners can see for themselves the quantities that the written forms represent. Carpentry, food preparation, and money provide familiar examples of concepts and procedures:

- The concept of a fraction of a whole can be shown by cutting up any objects such as pizzas or apples, real or drawn.
- Finding common denominators for adding and subtracting fractions, such as 1/4 minus 1/8, can be demonstrated with pieces of pizza, showing that 1/4 is the equivalent of 2/8.
- Rulers or measuring cups and spoons can show relative sizes of the different fractions such as halves versus sixteenths.
- Money can be used to show how the decimal system relates to other types of fractions: that 1/2, .5 or .50, and 50% are all the same, and that 1/4, .25, and 25% are all the same.

Learning to read fractions of an inch on a ruler or measuring tape is an example of a practical skill that helps with understanding the terminology and the written forms of fractions. They help to understand the relationship between halves, fourths, eighths, and sixteenths. This understanding is best achieved in two stages. First, learners can get hands-on experience in dividing real life objects into fractions and naming the pieces, and then they can learn how to divide and label a line into the same fractions.

The first set of activities could be:
- Folding and labeling sheets of brightly colored paper into halves, then fourths, then eighths and sixteenths.
- Slicing, naming and eating the same fractions of cakes, apples, oranges or chocolate bars.

Second, using the fraction lines of a tape measure or a ruler as a model, on a whiteboard or a piece of paper, the tutor and learner can:
- Construct a number line representing one inch (or a foot, or a yard). A number line larger than a real inch is easier to make divisions on.
- Compare both the 1/16 of the orange to the 1/16 on the number line to the whole of each, to reinforce what part 1/16 is to the whole.

Understanding and naming decimals: Place value in decimals follows the same pattern as place value in whole numbers. The only difference is that the value of digits increases tenfold each step to the right of the decimal point, instead of the left. Here are some examples of decimals and several different possible ways of naming them:

DECIMAL POINT	TENTHS	HUNDREDTHS	THOUSANDTHS	TEN THOUSANDTHS
.	3			
.	1	5		
.	0	7		
.	3	9	1	
.	0	0	0	3

The top number, stated in words, would be "point three" or "three tenths."

The next number would be "point one five," or "fifteen hundredths."

The one following that would be "point oh seven," "point zero seven," or "seven hundredths."

Next would be "point three nine one," or "three hundred ninety-one thousandths."

The last number would be "three ten-thousandths," or "point zero zero zero three."

The tutor and learner can look at this chart together, then practice writing and saying other examples. They should also compare the values of the decimals until the learner can sort decimals by size, watching especially how a zero to the immediate right of the decimal affects the value (.25 versus .025).

Percents are fractions expressing hundredths, often used to describe a portion of a large number, as in the following statistics:

There is at least one gun in 39% of US households, or 39 in every 100 households.

The candidate won 56% of the vote, or 56 of every 100 votes.

Buy our product now and save 10%, or ten hundredths of the price.

Percent fractions are written with a percent symbol at the end. Printed decimal points express fractions of percents. For example, decimals are converted to percents as follows:

.15 = 15%, or 15 out of 100.

.3 (or .30) = 30%, or 30 out of 100.

.07 = 7%, or 7 out of 100.

.391 = 39.1% or 39 and one tenth out of 100.

.0007 = .07% or 7 hundredths out of 100.

Using newspapers, goal-related materials, or materials from daily life, learners can read for understanding while converting the fractional quantities given into other equivalent forms, such as 20% into 1/5.

3. Reading graphs

Graphs present numerical information visually so as to simplify, reinforce, or emphasize it. Since they are used widely in popular newspapers and to accompany speeches and sales presentations, they have become an important element of reading comprehension. Graphs can take various forms, including these:

Circle graphs: Circle graphs represent a whole divided in segments like a slice of pie. They are easy to understand because the shape of the "pie slice" suggests its relative size.

Bar graphs: Vertical bars of different heights compare different quantities. They are clear as long as the reader knows the meaning of each bar, as well as its height.

Line graphs: A line connects points along vertical and horizontal axes. It is important to understand both the lines marking height and length. The horizontal axis often represents time, with the vertical axis representing a quantity being compared over time.

Picture graphs: Pictures or symbols are used to represent quantities. Population growth might be shown with human figures, one for every 10 million people.

With any type of graph, reading all of the information is vital to understanding the graph, paying close attention to titles, how the axes are labeled, and any keys to what the graphics (and units used) represent. For example, examine the following bar graph:

Thomas's Teddy Bears, Inc.

Regional Office Sales

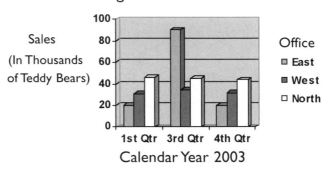

Sales (In Thousands of Teddy Bears)

Office
- East
- West
- North

Calendar Year 2003

The tutor and learner can determine from this graph the number of teddy bear sales which each office had in each quarter. This example can help them explore the many different graphs that the learner finds in his day-to-day life.

4. Mastering number facts

A learner may be able to work with double digit numbers, regrouping (carrying and borrowing), and maybe even long division, and yet not have all the addition, subtraction, multiplication and division facts, or "tables," memorized. Obviously, learners will be able to do math faster if they do not have to count on their fingers or look at multiplication tables, but they do not have to master these facts before working on the higher level computations. Working on nothing but memorizing the basic facts can become so boring that the learner loses concentration and actually learns less. Learners will remember more if they start working on challenging material while continuing to review basic facts.

Worksheets and flash cards: Worksheets such as the one illustrated earlier in this chapter, relating addition and subtraction, can help learners learn basic facts. The tutor can also make up worksheets on certain numbers, such as this one for 10, such an important number in our system:

Fill in the blanks to make 10.

6 + ___   5 + ___   9 + ___   8 + ___

3 + ___   4 + ___   5 + ___   1 + ___

How many tens are in each number?

30	300	130
70	700	170
20	200	120

Learners can also make their own flash cards for addition, subtraction, multiplication and division facts. Making them out of scratch paper or index cards is actually more educational than buying them. Learners will start memorizing as they write numbers on the cards, as well as when they use them to test themselves.

Games: If practicing flash cards gets monotonous, tutors and learners could use the same cards in bingo games. Here is how to do it:

- On 8 1/2 by 11 inch paper, draw a five-inch square containing twenty-five one-inch boxes.
- In these boxes, write the flash card numbers which will represent the flash card answers: sums, products, differences and quotients.
- One of the players draws flash cards and calls out the number combinations to be matched with the answers on the sheets of paper.
- Players use counters to cover the numbers, as in regular bingo.
- Tutors and learners can play against each other, and the games work even better with small groups of learners.

Concentration is another good game to help in memorizing number facts:

- Make two sets of cards, one with math combinations on them, such as 2 x 3, and another with the answers to the problems.
- Mix the two decks and lay the cards out in rows and columns.
- Each player takes a turn and turns over two cards.
- If the cards go together, the player keeps them and tries again.
- If they do not, the cards are turned back over and the next player takes a turn.

Calculators: Sometimes learners want to learn how to use calculators but think it would be cheating. They need to discover that calculators are useful tools for helping them become efficient and independent learners.

Many learners use calculators to drill themselves on basic facts this way:

- Press the buttons for the problem.
- Think of the answer.
- Check their response with the calculator.

Learners may need instruction in the sequence for pressing buttons, especially dividing, for which the larger number must be pressed first, because the symbol means "divided by," not "divided into."

Studying number facts by themselves may seem useful, but they are easily forgotten if they are not used in calculating material that is interesting and important to the learner. Tutors and learners must be careful not to get so involved with the small pieces of working on math that they take time away from the best way to learn, which is simply to do meaningful, goal-related work with numbers every day.

E. Putting It All Together

This section discusses how to help learners see the connections between adding, subtracting, multiplying and dividing; how to find materials for more advanced topics; and how to combine the necessary practice with helpful feedback.

1. Relationships between operations

Although most math workbooks teach the basic operations of addition, subtraction, multiplication and division separately, learners benefit by seeing the relationships between these operations. This knowledge will enhance their understanding of math, including their ability to work with fractions, geometry and other topics.

Understanding how the operations relate to each other will also help them with their daily use of numbers, such as measurement or money. To relate operations, tutors can present easy examples of addition and subtraction facts together. For example:

$$4 + 1 = 5 \qquad 1 + 4 = 5$$
$$5 - 1 = 4 \qquad 5 - 4 = 1$$

or:

$$4 + 2 = 6 \qquad 2 + 4 = 6$$
$$6 - 2 = 4 \qquad 6 - 4 = 2$$

Together, these statements reveal several mathematical concepts. Learners can see the commutativity of addition (the order doesn't matter), and the relationship between addition and subtraction. Without this type of exploration, learners are likely to see 4 + 1 and 1 + 4 as separate problems, working them out individually even when they are presented close together. When learners understand the relations between operations, work on memorization of basic numbers facts will be easier.

Learners are helped by seeing relationships between addition and multiplication. Multiplication is repeated addition:

$$3 \times 4 = 12 \quad \text{is the same as} \quad 4 + 4 + 4 = 12$$

Division is repeated subtraction, so 4 can be subtracted from 12 three times. $12 \div 4 = 3$ can be thought of as:

```
  12
  -4
   8
  -4
   4
  -4
   0
```

In order to add fractions with unlike denominators, such as 1/3 + 1/8, it is also necessary to do multiplication, division and addition.

To divide efficiently, it is necessary to move quickly between division, multiplication and subtraction. The estimation required to do the first step in a division problem, the dividing, is easily done by someone who knows the multiplication facts and understands that division is the reverse of multiplication. The next step, the subtracting, is easily done by the person who understands that subtraction is the operation for finding differences, in this case the difference between the result of multiplication and the number to be divided. Developing learners' flexibility will help make their numbers work more efficient and satisfying.

Because operations are interrelated, as we have seen, there is no need to keep plugging away at memorization of one operation, such as addition, before beginning work on another. Addition and subtraction facts can be learned together, and there is no harm in moving on to multiplication, after the concept of addition is understood. Additional practice in using addition facts can be gained while doing two-place multiplication, such as:

```
   32
 x 45
```

Working with a variety of operations is more interesting, and it prepares people for the complexity of the numbers situations occurring in real life.

2. What about more complicated math operations?

This section has presented guidelines for tutors to work with and understand numbers in general. Space does not permit a guide to all of the various procedures included in mathematical operations. There are a variety of resources which can be used by learners and tutors who plan to use higher level materials. Tutors and their coordinators at Center for Literacy have found Contemporary's *Number Power* series to be helpful when providing a structured approach to math tutoring. Many other materials are accessible over the Internet.

When working with more challenging material, it is especially important to keep track of the meaning and application of math procedures and calculations. In each session, learners and tutors need to look at the relationship between the numerical learning and the real world and think about how this learning can help the learner do the things that she wants to.

3. Practice and feedback

When adults work toward meeting their math goals, they need both practice and feedback. One way to get practice is for learners to make up their own problems which has these benefits:

- It provides the learner with the satisfaction of control over learning activities.
- It paces learning appropriately, since the learner is the best person to find problems in the range between being meaninglessly easy and impossibly hard.
- It connects math learning with the learners' lives.

Understanding the learner's thinking: Learners' practice needs to be monitored, either by themselves or their tutor. While learners are working during their sessions, tutors need to observe them without interruption as they work through problems. It is very helpful for learners to think out loud as they work. This can be difficult, especially the first few times, but it is worth the effort. The tutor can also ask the learner to explain a problem to him. Hearing learners' explanations can reveal their degree of understanding as well as any misconceptions.

For example, learners may say that a piece of paper cut once, then cut again, will consist of four halves. They may explain that each piece of paper was cut in half, revealing that they assign the name "half" in relation to the piece last cut (actually a fourth), not in relation to the original piece.

When a tutor sees a learner use an incorrect procedure, it is helpful for the tutor to wait and see if the learner makes related mistakes, in which case it is likely to be the result of a misunderstanding, rather than simply carelessness. Relearning one thing that was learned incorrectly will save a lot of time in the future. For instance, if the learner had done this:

$$
\begin{array}{r} 3 \\ +\ 2 \\ \hline 6 \end{array}
\qquad\qquad
\begin{array}{r} 3 \\ \times\ 2 \\ \hline 5 \end{array}
$$

the tutor who looked at the work would have seen that the error was in confusing the symbols for adding and multiplying. This fact would have been overlooked if the tutor had simply checked the answers.

A learner might show confusion in doing this problem:

The learner has done the subtraction in the ones column correctly, but regrouped from the hundreds place without recording any change in the tens place. If the tutor takes time to discuss the problems with the learner, observe the learner's process, and correct misunderstandings, it will be easier to make progress.

$$\begin{array}{r} 302 \\ -\ 8 \\ \hline 204 \end{array}$$

IV. SOME QUESTIONS AND ANSWERS ABOUT MATH

These responses of a coordinator to concerns about math expressed by tutors and learners may be useful:

Q: The learners seem to understand the explanation during the session, but when they try to do similar problems at home, they've forgotten.

A: Practicing several problems during the session, right after the explanation, is important. It is important to be sure the learners really understand and are not merely remembering procedures. It's best if learners try to work at home as soon as possible after the session, while their memories are fresh. Another possibility is to have a "math buddy" they can call up if they have a question.

Q: How can we find time to do math as well as reading and writing?

A: Time is always a problem. One possibility is to work on math one day of the week, and reading and writing on the other. Another is to do problems that involve reading and writing, such as getting ideas from the newspaper, as described in this chapter. Plan carefully, keeping in mind the learner's goals.

Q: The learners don't like looking up answers in the back of the book or using calculators because it feels like cheating.

A: These feelings come from school, where the teacher was in charge of the learning. Adult learning is different because the learners are in charge and should take responsibility for checking their own answers whenever possible.

The tutor can explain that his role is to help learners understand the material, not just check answers. Calculators and answer pages are useful tools for enabling learners to become independent learners.

V. CONCLUSION

Working with numbers provides an interesting variation from working with words. As learners connect their new learning to their daily lives, their sense of competence grows. Knowledge is power, as much with numbers, as with words.

Chapter 8

Assessment and Planning

Assessment and planning are done when learners enter literacy programs, and continue after learners have been working with tutors for a while to evaluate what has been accomplished so far and plan what should be done next.

In this chapter, we describe how literacy needs and progress can be assessed by literacy agency staff, as well as by tutors and learners, through conferences, learning logs, portfolios, and informal conversation. We also make recommendations for long-range planning and offer guidelines for planning lessons for the immediate future, for individuals and small groups in all aspects of literacy. We also present specific sample lesson plans for basic literacy learners at two different levels and for a small intermediate English as a second language (ESL) group.

I. ASSESSMENT

A. Initial Assessment

Because learners and tutors need to know where to begin, most adult literacy providing agencies conduct an initial assessment when learners first enroll in the program. Center for Literacy, for example, has developed three procedures for discovering learners' goals, strengths and learning needs: standardized testing as required by its primary funding agency; its one-to-one or small group planning conference done by an agency staff member; and its Goals Checklist, described in Chapter 2, which is used by staff during the conference and by learners and tutors during their first sessions. We offer the planning conference and Goals Checklist as examples of effective assessment strategies which other agencies might adapt for their own situation.

1. The Center for Literacy Initial Planning Conference

Upon entering the CFL program, learners meet with the area coordinator for the Initial Planning Conference to discuss their literacy goals, skills, needs, and interests.

In this interview, coordinators first explore the place of reading, writing and math in the learners' lives by discussing:

- What brought them to the program.
- How they use reading and writing now.
- What specific uses of reading and writing they want to improve.
- Their ideas about what makes a person a good reader and writer.
- Whether they want to work on math, and if so, on what topics.
- The learning needs and priorities of ESL.

During the same interview, the coordinator does the following to assess each learner's abilities and needs:

- Asks the learner to do a series of increasingly challenging tasks of reading, writing, and math or speaking English, if applicable, stopping at the point where the learner shows signs of frustration.
- Begins the process of instruction by discussing the learner's skills and ideas about reading, writing, and math or speaking English, if applicable.
- Evaluates the learner's reading, writing, and math or English, if applicable, in terms of uses, understanding, strategies, and ability to use the assistance provided by the coordinator.
- Writes a summary of the learner's goals, strategies, strengths and needs.
- Writes recommendations for instruction, including specific materials and activities.

Through this planning conference, learners realize what they are able to do. They often remark at the end of the interview that they found they knew more than they thought they did. The written summary and recommendations are intended to guide the learner and tutor during their first sessions together.

2. The Center for Literacy Goals Checklist

The Goals Checklist, described in Chapter 2, "Literacy and Adult Learning," helps learners think of things that might not have occurred to them. It is especially useful for getting started. The checklist allows the learners to tell what they can do, what they want to work on, what they are making progress on, and what they have no interest in, giving them a chance to tell of their strengths, as well as their wishes.

B. Assessing Progress

Adults who have decided to improve their reading and writing need to see their own progress and know they that are not wasting their time. They may come with many self-doubts, and, if they do not see progress fairly soon, may feel that any self-doubts they brought to the sessions have been confirmed. If they leave, they may lose not only an opportunity to learn, but also some of their self-esteem.

Progress can be assessed through the agency's regular procedures and during the sessions, much of it an ongoing process that people do naturally. For example, learners and tutors often note progress by comparing present work to earlier work. In addition to such informal observation, it is helpful for tutors and learners to set a regular routine for assessment.

1. Planning Conference II

At CFL, staff members conduct an interview approximately six months after the beginning of their tutoring sessions. The coordinator meets each learner-tutor pair or small group for the Planning Conference II to make sure that the program is meeting each learner's needs. Together, the coordinator, the tutor and learner:

- Look at the learner's portfolios and learning logs.
- Assess the learner's progress and satisfaction.
- Discuss plans for the next few months.
- Arrange for new materials, after discussing materials and activities.
- Check on whether learner goals are being met, and whether they have changed as learning progresses.
- Look over recent lesson plans to re-evaluate the balance of activities and the pace of the lessons.

2. Learning logs

What is a learning log? A learning log is a journal in which tutor and learner together write what was done, learned and enjoyed in each session, and record their plans for the future. Learning logs are useful for these reasons:

- They provide a record of what was worked on and learned.
- They help with remembering newly learned material.
- They get learners and tutors started on planning future sessions.

How is it written? At the end of each session, learners and tutors talk together and then write a few sentences about:

- What was done.
- How hard it was.

- How successful they were.
- How they felt about it.
- What was learned.

Either the learners or the tutor can do the writing, or learners in turn might dictate the log to the tutor. They can also plan the next lesson at this time and read it at the beginning of the next session.

The following is an example of a few learning log entries of a small group of three learners and a tutor:

Note: Grace, Gloria and Lisa are basic literacy learners. Ann is the tutor. They wrote their log together at the end of each session. Sometimes the learners told the tutor what to write, and sometimes Gloria or Lisa did the writing while the others made suggestions.

July 31

We wrote for four minutes, then read the stories to each other. Grace wrote about her sister's new house. Lisa wrote about her boyfriend, and Gloria wrote about how her children are getting on her nerves. Ann wrote about finding enough time. We looked at the words we worked on last week, and talked about writing at home every day, even if it's hard to get started.Grace picked out part of the driver's manual for Ann to make a tape recording from, to read along with at home. Lisa and Gloria made their grocery shopping lists from the newspaper.

August 11

Grace wrote about her catering job. Gloria wrote about the hospital, and Lisa wrote about her neighbor's dog. We took turns reading *The Life of Lucy Fern*, with Grace echo reading after Gloria. We talked about who should get the baby. We made a list of words spelled with *th* and *ough*, and talked about their meanings and put them on cards to study *(through, tough, though, thought)*. Next time we'll do calculations with money and counting change.

September 14

We read *A Dream With Storms*. Grace did echo reading after Lisa. Lisa helped Gloria write a letter to Kevin's teacher. Grace dictated a story about a wedding to Ann, then Ann helped her read the story back to her. Grace picked words from her story to put on cards and study at home. Lisa and Gloria tested each other on their spelling lists. We talked about how to write money in decimals and practiced adding money when some of it is in cents and some is in dollars.

3. Portfolios

What are they? A portfolio is a collection of the learner's best work, selected by the learner. The portfolio can be any collection of work that she chooses, such as:

- Examples of writing.
- Lists of books read.
- Lists or copies of calculations done, such as balancing a checkbook.

Or it can record evidence of success, such as:

- Passing the driver's test.
- Speaking up at the Home and School Association meeting.

Why use portfolios? Like learning logs, they are a real and satisfying way of showing what has been accomplished over time. They offer these advantages:

- They are more realistic than tests for showing what a person is able to do because, unlike most tests, they are a normal-length sample of the learner's work done in relaxed circumstances.
- They empower the learners because they are the ones who choose the material to put into them.
- They help learners keep track of what they have learned.
- Looking at the portfolio at regular intervals provides valuable information about successes and needs for further work.

How do you make them?

- The learner's name is written on a folder with pockets.
- Every week or two the learner selects a piece of work for the folder. The work can be a favorite, the most challenging, or one at which the learner felt particularly successful:

> Pieces of writing.
>
> Titles of articles and books read.
>
> Goal-related materials such as job applications.
>
> Evidence of success, such as passing the driver's test.
>
> A project involving mathematics.

- The date is written on every piece.
- Learning logs can be included.

How do you use them? Tutors and learners can assess progress by comparing recent work with what was done earlier, asking the following questions:

- How many topics were there for writing, and how long are the pieces?
- How clear, detailed and lively is the writing?
- How many materials were read, and how hard were they?
- How many numeracy tasks were done, and how hard were they?
- How many ESL tasks were done, and how hard were they?

Looking over the logs, they can also check for changes:

- How fluently does the learner seem to read these materials?
- Does the learner monitor her own comprehension when reading?
- Does she revise her own writing?
- Can she make up her own number problems and solve them?
- How is her English communication?
- How willing is the learner to take on challenging material and activities?

4. Talking about changes in habits and attitudes

Talking about learners' literacy learning activities outside of the sessions, doing reading, writing, speaking English, or numeracy, is another important way to assess the impact of the tutoring. Tutors can ask, "What are you doing now, in the areas we've been working on, that you couldn't or didn't do before?" Learners may report changes in activities and attitudes:

- One learner began reading the newspaper every day because she wanted to find out more details.
- A learner wrote a letter to a public official instead of telephoning because he could think carefully about what to say and how.
- A learner designed a bookcase and ordered lumber cut to the size he wanted.
- Learners' children became more willing to do their homework because they saw their mother studying.
- An ESL learner now feels comfortable answering the phone when it rings and doesn't wait for her children pick it up.

Changes in attitudes may be more important than any growth in skills, because their effect on future learning will be more lasting.

C. Celebration of Success

Assessment provides the opportunity for celebration, in print or at public events. Learners and tutors alike appreciate being recognized for their efforts. For example, the Center for Literacy does the following:

- Its newsletter, *The CFL Letter*, features learners' success stories, which are sent in by tutors and learners, including all or only part of the learner's name, as they prefer.

- The annual Speak Out event provides learners with the opportunity to read their own writings in public and see them in a printed book.

- The annual recognition event celebrates success in participating in the program. Outstanding learners are honored, and all who attend are awarded a certificate of recognition.

In all these ways, success was defined by the learner's own goals, including success in meeting standards set by others, such as passing the driver's test or the GED.

II. LESSON PLANNING

What is lesson planning? Lesson planning involves deciding and writing down what to study, and what materials and activities to use. It includes long-range plans for weeks or months ahead and short-range lesson plans for sessions within the next week or two. Lesson plans should be flexible, reflecting the learners' views of their own needs which may change over the weeks.

Who should do it? Lesson planning should be done by learners and tutors together because tutors and learners each bring their own knowledge. The tutors may know more about reading and writing, but the learners know more about their own needs, interests and ways of learning.

How are plans helpful? Lesson plans are reminders to the tutor and learner of what to do, making sure that one activity isn't pushing others aside. Even when plans are later changed, tutors who write down their plans in advance proceed with more confidence. Lesson plans also can be useful during the next assessment, as a supplement to the learning logs.

A. Making Long-Range Lesson Plans

Long-range plans covering several weeks usually cover broad topics, with a few materials and activities as examples. They are made with the understanding that the pace and the sequence of topics may change as well as the materials and activities.

Achieving a balance:

What should be in the long-term plans? When planning for several weeks, learners and tutors need to think about the larger picture. Tutors and learners can look over their list of goals, select one or more short-term goals, and decide which materials and activities to use to achieve it. Over the weeks, the sessions should include a balance of:

- Reading connected prose for information and pleasure.
- Writing connected prose for real-life purposes.
- Speaking and listening to communicate in English for ESL learners.
- Understanding and applying numbers concepts, if numeracy is part of the learner's goals.
- Opportunistic teaching: developing and practicing strategies for skills, improving recognition, spelling and understanding of words, or working with numbers, or doing English language or pronunciation exercises.

Elements of literacy combined: Whenever possible, it is helpful to relate areas such as reading, writing, numbers and speaking, to each other to make activities more realistic and ease transitions from one activity to another.

Old and new learning combined: Every lesson should include "something old and something new." Review and repetition are essential for remembering so new material needs to be combined with variations on what was studied before. Instruction needs to be balanced between the review needed for remembering and new material for interest and a sense of progress.

B. Planning Individual Sessions

1. What should short-term plans include?

Plans for the next week or so are most useful when they are detailed and specific and include the goals for the lesson; the materials and activities to be done, showing the sequence; and the estimated time for each activity. As with long-range plans, they should be adaptable to the learners' changes in interests and concerns and open to opportunistic teaching of skills, based on needs as they arise.

2. When should you make short-range plans?

It is often easiest to make detailed plans for the next session right after writing the learning log.

3. What is the best way to divide the time in a session?

Individuals vary in how long they want to work on one thing, and tutors and learners soon develop a sense of how much time to allow. The times given here are rough guides, but, for an hour-and-a-half lesson, the time might be divided this way:

For basic literacy:

- Five minutes discussing their uses of reading and writing since the last session.
- Half an hour reading, including preparation and discussion.
- Ten minutes of skills instruction and practice, based on needs revealed while reading.
- Half an hour writing, including planning, sharing, getting responses and revising.
- Ten minutes of skills instruction and practice, based on needs revealed in the writing.
- Five minutes for writing a learning log at the end.

For numeracy: When numeracy is also one of the goals, the arrangement described above could combine the reading and writing activities, and add the following:

- Twenty minutes planning a math project, such as measuring or calculating interest.
- Twenty minutes practicing the operations needed in the project, such as adding fractions or multiplying by decimals.

For ESL: ESL learners usually want to spend most of their time on speaking and listening, with some reading and writing. They could do the following:

- Five minutes discussing the conversations and other activities they did since the last session.
- Twenty minutes of role-playing.
- Ten minutes of practice exercises on pronunciation.
- Twenty minutes of conversation.

- Twenty minutes of dictating or writing a related language experience story, reading and discussing it.
- Ten minutes of exercises on vocabulary, American idioms and slang or grammatical structures.
- Five minutes writing a learning log.

For groups: Alternating between whole-group and individuals or pairs: The examples given above for all aspects of literacy can be adapted for small groups of one tutor and three to five learners, which are particularly recommended for ESL learners. The plans should allow for a combination of whole-group activity and work in smaller groups or alone. The sessions could begin and end with a whole-group period, each about twenty minutes long. These are the benefits of the whole-group part of the sessions:

- Opening as a whole group lets people enjoy belonging to a community of learners
- Closing as a group lets people look at the day's work and plan for future sessions
- Whole group activities let people learn from each other.

For the fifty minutes in the middle, the tutor can work with different learners in turn, alone or in pairs, to meet their differing needs, while the others work alone or with others.

4. Specific examples of lesson plans

The example of a learning log given earlier in this chapter describes one set of specific materials and activities, and now we offer some more detailed suggestions for lesson plans. Again, the times given are rough guides, and may vary from the suggestions in the previous section. We refer to learning activities described in earlier chapters.

For a basic level literacy learner: This plan combines reading, writing, and numeracy. The learner has a short term goal of learning to read labels on some medicine containers he brought from home, and he also wants to work on basic arithmetic.

Reading and Writing:
Discuss reading and writing done at home. (5 min.)

Read the medicine labels, using echo reading, followed by assisted oral reading. (20 min.)

Write words from the labels on cards and study them as sight words or analyze their syllables. (10 min.)

Dictate a story about taking care of a sick child, using names of medicines; then read the story with tutor, then alone. (30 min.)

Make cards of, and read, selected words from the story. (10 min.)

Numbers: (15 min.)
Calculate how many pills are taken per day, then per week, at the rate of one every four hours.

Learning Log: (5 min.)
Write a learning log together.

For more advanced literacy learners: More advanced learners who want to be able to read novels for pleasure and to write essays for the GED test might do the following:

Review: (5 min.)
Discuss reading and writing done outside the session.

Reading: (30 min.)
Discuss the story so far, predicting what you think will happen next.
Read half the selection orally, in turn, pausing to signal the next reader to take over, then read silently *The Life of Lucy Fern*.
Discuss why the different characters in the story want to adopt the baby.

Reading skills: (10 min.)
Discuss any unknown meanings of words, and decoding by syllable, of any words that gave difficulty in recognizing.

Writing: (30 min.)
After discussion, write an essay on how adoption decisions should be made.
Read the essay aloud, discuss, revise.

Writing skills: (10 min.)
Work on punctuation as needed: explanation followed by practice (for example, 's to show possession).

Learning Log: (5 min.)
Write a learning log together.

For ESL learners: This plan is for three intermediate learners who work in a restaurant. They read and write English quite well, but they have difficulty understanding it in noisy settings, and sometimes people don't understand what they say. They want to know more idioms and slang and meet young people their age.

Review: (5 min.)
Discuss speaking and listening experiences at work since the last session.

Speaking and listening experience: (15 min.)
Role play dealing with a customer who got dressing on her salad when she had asked for it on the side.

Pronunciation exercises: (10 min.)
Practice stressing the right syllable, using menu items and other restaurant vocabulary, such as reservation.
Minimum contrast pairs for /i/ and /ee/ sounds: I fill the shopping bag; I feel good.

Speaking and listening experience: (15 min.)
Conversation about social customs among young people here and in their native country.

Writing and reading: (20 min.)
After discussion, write or dictate a story about a social event in their native country. Read the stories aloud, discuss, revise.

Listening exercise: (10 min.)
Back-to-back telephone conversation inviting somebody to a party and giving directions.

Grammar and fluency exercise: (10 min.)
Practice past and future tense with drills starting with yesterday and tomorrow. Make one of these sentences longer and practice backward buildup.

Learning Log: (5 min.)
Write a learning log together.

III. CONCLUSION

Assessment and planning allow tutors and learners to make the most of their time together, knowing exactly why they are doing any activity with any material. Assessments may not always be accurate, but they provide a starting point. Plans are always subject to change, but having them provides both a starting point and a sense of security.

Chapter 9

Maintaining Progress

To conclude this handbook, we would like to consider a few important ways that tutors and learners can keep the learning moving along successfully. They need to meet their ongoing needs for materials, stay in touch, and get help when factors outside of literacy learning threaten to interfere with their literacy learning. Here are some suggestions for meeting these needs:

I. GETTING MATERIALS

Literacy agencies have a variety of resources for materials. Libraries are one of the most valuable, and many literacy programs are in fact supported by libraries. Every literacy learner should be encouraged to get a library card. A trip to the library helps learners know where to look for what they want, as well as helping learners to feel comfortable about going.

When tutors and learners talk together about learner goals, they will think of other ways to get materials. Learners and tutors can bring things from their own homes at any time. When tutors become attuned to learners' interests, they will find relevant material every time they read a newspaper or magazine. Learners, too, can get in the habit of seeing anything, whether a grocery receipt or a contract they need to sign, as possible learning materials.

II. STAYING IN TOUCH

Tutors and learners: Nothing is more discouraging to learners or to tutors than to get to their meeting place and not have their partners show up. Learners and tutors need to be able to reach each other if anything should come up to prevent their meeting. They need to have each other's phone numbers recorded in more than one place. If a person has no phone, he should give the phone number of a neighbor or a family member who would relay a message.

Tutors, learners, and staff: If problems arise in the tutoring, an agency staff person should be consulted. Staff members are experienced in dealing with instructional issues, including giving supplies, performing assessments, suggesting teaching strategies, and helping find meeting places. They are also experienced in making referrals to other agencies for problems beyond their expertise.

Outside support: The tutor may become concerned about serious problems in the learner's personal life. Although the tutor should show support and concern, it is not the tutor's responsibility to provide services other than literacy instruction. Coordinators can meet learners' needs through referrals to outside agencies. Tutors are most helpful when they stay focused on their role of giving learners the reading, writing, English and numeracy help they request.

III. CONCLUSION

Throughout this handbook, we have presented our beliefs that literacy learning helps people enrich and control their own lives. The experience of working together for a shared goal, with people they might not otherwise have met, can be deep and satisfying. Both tutors and learners gain as they learn each other's point of view. Tutors get

a deeper understanding of how literacy learning weaves into people's lives, and learners develop new goals, such as reading for pleasure, as they see how their lives are changed by learning.

We wish the pleasure and satisfaction of achievement to the tutors and learners for whom this handbook was written. We hope they meet all their goals, and that the learners decide to come back some day as tutors.

New Instant Word List

By Edward Fry

The first 10 words make up about 24% of all written material.
The 100 words make up about 50% of all written material.

THE FIRST HUNDRED

Group 1a	Group 1b	Group 1c	Group 1d
the	or	will	number
of	one	up	no
and	had	other	way
a	by	about	could
to	word	out	people
in	but	many	my
is	not	then	than
you	what	them	first
that	all	these	water
it	were	so	been
he	we	some	call
was	when	her	who
for	your	would	oil
on	can	make	now
are	said	like	find
as	there	him	long
with	use	into	down
his	an	time	day
they	each	has	did
I	which	look	get
at	she	two	come
be	do	more	made
this	how	write	may
have	their	go	part
from	if	see	over

Reprinted with permission of Edward Fry and the International Reading Association from *The Reading Teacher*, December, 1980.

Writing Ideas

I. IDEAS FOR STORIES

- A sixteen-year-old girl is sitting in her parents' living room struggling to find the right words to tell her parents that she is pregnant. Or, it could be a boy trying to tell his parents that he is about to become a father.

- A five-year-old child is sitting in a darkened bedroom, convinced that there is a nasty monster on the other side of his/her bedroom door.

- A customer service representative in a department store is standing behind the courtesy counter. An angry customer walks up to the desk screaming and waving a receipt. The customer service representative is trying quickly to decide how to handle this situation.

- A grandparent who has been poor all of his/her life has just won ten million dollars in the lottery and is now trying to decide what to do with it.

- The President of the United States is in the Oval Office on his/her first day of service, deciding what to do first.

- These scenes can be written from the point of view of different people. Each could be written in the first person, ("I sat there...") or as seen by an observer. A writer may write the same scene more than once, from different points of view.

II. IDEAS FOR WRITING A DESCRIPTIVE ESSAY

Vivid writing: Good writing brings a scene to life by using details, often from one or more of the five senses. Writers can use sentences like these to start a descriptive paragraph, using as many sensory impressions as possible to make the experience seem real.

- "Thanksgiving dinner was unbelievable."
- "I never have gotten used to winter."
- "He could remember every detail of his grandmother's kitchen."
- "The garbage dump was especially noticeable in summer."
- "Our street gets noisier by late afternoon."
- "When I entered the building for my first interview, I could feel the butterflies in my stomach."
- "I remember the joy I felt when the doctor told me it was a boy!"

Explaining a process: This kind of writing gives learners a chance to share their knowledge with others. They need to be clear, and to present steps in logical order. Here are some possible topics:

- How is your favorite game played?
- How do you change the oil in a car?
- Can you share your favorite recipe?
- What are some painless ways to save money?
- How do you get a date with someone you really like?
- How can you smooth things out after a stupid argument?

III. 50 JOURNAL TOPICS

Since some of these are of a deeply personal nature, you don't have to talk about what you write, nor will anyone else see your writing. Don't concern yourself with spelling and punctuation. Rather, try to describe each topic in its fullest detail. If you can't think of something, make it up! Record how many minutes it took.

Describe a simple pleasure in your life.
Time written: _____
Words written: _____
Date written: _____

When you were small, who were your heroes? Why?
Time written: _____   Words written: _____   Date written: _____

What person today do you admire most? Why?
Time written: _____   Words written: _____   Date written: _____

Tell about a time you got in trouble (under age 18).
Time written: _____   Words written: _____   Date written: _____

Tell about a childhood injury.
Time written: _____   Words written: _____   Date written: _____

What was the best thing about your neighborhood when you were young?
Time written: _____   Words written: _____   Date written: _____

How would a parent describe you as a child?
Time written: _____
Words written: _____
Date written: _____

Describe something you did to tease a brother or sister?
Time written: _____
Words written: _____
Date written: _____

How do you feel about returning to education right now?
Time written: _____
Words written: _____
Date written: _____

Name something you hate to do. Why?
Time written: _____
Words written: _____
Date written: _____

If you could have one wish come true, what would it be? Why?
Time written: _____   Words written: _____   Date written: _____

What is there about you that makes your friends like you? Why?
Time written: _____   Words written: _____   Date written: _____

What is the greatest disappointment that you have ever had?
Time written: _____   Words written: _____   Date written: _____

If your home were on fire, what five things (besides your family) would you save and why?
Time written: _____   Words written: _____   Date written: _____

What inscription would you put on a gravestone? Why?
Time written: _____   Words written: _____   Date written: _____

What kind of situation would you like to be in ten years from now?
Time written: _____   Words written: _____   Date written: _____

If you could live one day of your life over, which would it be? Why?
Time written: _____   Words written: _____   Date written: _____

What is a major accomplishment in your life so far?
Time written: _____   Words written: _____   Date written: _____

What is something you've learned in life so far?
Time written: _____   Words written: _____   Date written: _____

How would your friends have described
you in elementary school?
Time written: _____
Words written: _____
Date written: _____

What would the ideal child be like?
Time written: _____
Words written: _____
Date written: _____

What would the ideal set of parents be like?
Time written: _____   Words written: _____   Date written: _____

Have you ever faced death? Describe the experience.
Time written: _____   Words written: _____   Date written: _____

If this were your birthday, and you were your best friend/lover, what would you
give yourself?
Time written: _____   Words written: _____   Date written: _____

What was the best gift that you ever received? Why?
Time written: _____   Words written: _____   Date written: _____

What is the best thing that has happened to you in the past twenty-four hours?
Time written: _____   Words written: _____   Date written: _____

Describe everything you saw on the way to the session today.
Time written: _____   Words written: _____   Date written: _____

If you could be talented in something
that you are not talented in right now,
what would it be? Why?
Time written: _____
Words written: _____
Date written: _____

If you could teach everyone in the world just one thing, what would it be? Why?
Time written: _____   Words written: _____   Date written: _____

What is the worst job you ever had? Why?
Time written: _____   Words written: _____   Date written: _____

What is your most irrational fear? Describe a time when you had to confront it.
Time written: _____   Words written: _____   Date written: _____

What is your favorite "pig out" food?
Time written: _____   Words written: _____   Date written: _____

What is the worst advice someone ever gave you? How so?
Time written: _____   Words written: _____   Date written: _____

If you could change one thing about yourself, what would it be? Why?
Time written: _____   Words written: _____   Date written: _____

What is the most important thing you can teach a child?
Time written: _____   Words written: _____   Date written: _____

Describe yourself as your best friend would describe you.
Time written: _____   Words written: _____   Date written: _____

What are the three nicest things that other people have said to you?
Time written: _____   Words written: _____   Date written: _____

Describe the best friend of all time. What was the best time you had together?
Time written: _____
Words written: _____
Date written: _____

What are some things that make you unique?
Time written: _____
Words written: _____

Date written: _____

If you could live in another time in history, what time would you choose to live? Why?
Time written: _____
Words written: _____
Date written: _____

Write about the worst, weirdest, or funniest dream you ever had.
Time written: _____   Words written: _____   Date written: _____

If you won ten million dollars in the lottery, what would you do with it?
Time written: _____   Words written: _____   Date written: _____

Write about a disagreement you had with another person.
Time written: _____   Words written: _____   Date written: _____

What things irritate you the most? How do people know when you are angry?
Time written: _____   Words written: _____   Date written: _____

What five things would you put in a time capsule that would tell people in the future the most important things about you and the time in which you lived? Why?
Time written: _____   Words written: _____   Date written: _____

Write about a time you told a lie that you later either regretted or did not regret.
Time written: _____   Words written: _____   Date written: _____

Write a letter to yourself from a relative no longer living.
Time written: _____   Words written: _____   Date written: _____

If you could come back as anything (plant, animal, or human), what would you choose? Why?
Time written: _____   Words written: _____   Date written: _____

How would you go about persuading a child to stay in school?
Time written: _____   Words written: _____   Date written: _____

What is your greatest hope for the future?
Time written: _____   Words written: _____   Date written: _____

Fraction/Decimal/Percent Conversion Table

Conversion Rules:

1. Converting a decimal to a percent: move the decimal 2 places to the right and add % sign;
2. Converting a percent to a decimal: move the decimal 2 places to the left and drop the % sign;
3. Converting a fraction to a decimal or a percent: divide the whole into the part and follow decimal rule above.
4. Converting a percent to decimal to a decimal: divide percent by 100 over 1.

Fraction	Decimal	Percent
1/2	0.50	50%
1/3	0.33	33 1/3%
2/3	0.67	66 2/3%
1/4	0.25	25%
3/4	0.75	75%
1/5	0.20	20%
2/5	0.40	40%
3/5	0.60	60%

Multiplication Tables

	0	1	2	3	4	5	6	7	8	9	10	11	12
0	0	0	0	0	0	0	0	0	0	0	0	0	0
1	0	1	2	3	4	5	6	7	8	9	10	11	12
2	0	2	4	6	8	10	12	14	16	18	20	22	24
3	0	3	6	9	12	15	18	21	24	27	30	33	36
4	0	4	8	12	16	20	24	28	32	36	40	44	48
5	0	5	10	15	20	25	30	35	40	45	50	55	60
6	0	6	12	18	24	30	36	42	48	54	60	66	72
7	0	7	14	21	28	35	42	49	56	63	70	77	84
8	0	8	16	24	32	40	48	56	64	72	80	88	96
9	0	9	18	27	36	45	54	63	72	81	90	99	108
10	0	10	20	30	40	50	60	70	80	90	100	110	120
11	0	11	22	33	44	55	66	77	88	99	110	121	132
12	0	12	24	36	48	60	72	84	96	108	120	132	144

Bibliography

Allen, J. (2004). *Tools for teaching content literacy.* Portland, ME: Stenhouse Publishers.

American Council On Education (2002). *Information bulletin on the tests of general educational development.* Washington, DC: Author.

Belzer, A. (2004). "It's not like normal school": The role of prior learning contexts in adult learning. *Adult Education Journal,* 55(1), 41-59.

Bishop, D. V. M., & Snowling, M. J. (2004). Developmental dyslexia and specific language impairment: Same or different? *Psychological Bulletin* by the American Psychological Association, 130(6), 858-886.

Blomert, L., Mitterer, H., & Paffen, C. (2004). In search of the auditory, phonetic, and/or phonological problems in dyslexia: Context effects in speech perception. *Journal of Speech, Language, and Hearning Research,* 47, 1030-1047.

Boden, C., & Brodeur, D. A. (1999). Visual processing of verbal and nonverbal stimuli in adolescents with reading disabilities. *Journal of Learning Disabilities,* 32(1), 58-71.

Campbell, P. (2003). *Teaching reading to adults a balanced approach.* Edmonton, Alberta: Grass Roots Press.

Cross, P. (1984). *Adults as learners.* San Francisco: Jossey-Bass.

Curtis, M.E. & Kruidenier, J. (2005). *A summary of scientifically based research principles teaching adults to read.* Washington, DC: National Institute for Literacy.

Cutting, L. E., & Denckla, M. B. (2001). The relationship of rapid serial naming and word reading in normally developing readers: An exploratory model. *Reading and Writing: An Interdisciplinary Journal,* 14, 673-705.

Freire, P. (1999). *Pedagogy of the oppressed.* New York: The Continuum Publishing Company. (Original work published 1921)

Fry, E. B., Kress, J. E., & Fountoukidis, D. L. (2000). *The reading teacher's book of lists (4th).* Paramus, NJ: Prentice Hall.

Goswami, U. (2000). Phonological and lexical processes. In M. Kamil, P. B. Mosenthal, P. D. Pearson & R. Barr (Vols. Ed.), *Handbook of Reading Research* (III, pp. 251-267). Mahwah, NJ: Lawrence Erlbaum Associates.

Hill, L. H., & Brockett, R. G. (Eds.). (2001). Adult learners with disabilities - An overlooked population. *Adult Learning,* 12(2).

Kazemek, F. E., & Rigg, P. (1995). *Enriching our lives: Poetry lessons for adult literacy teachers and tutors*. Newark, DE: International Reading Association.

Kruidenier, J. (2002). *Research-based principles for adult basic education reading instruction*. Washington, DC: National Institute for Literacy.

Massengill, D. (2004). The impact of using guided reading to teach low-literate adults. *Journal of Adolescent & Adult Literacy, 47*(7), 588-602.

National Adult Literacy and Learning Disability Center. (1999). *Bridges to practice: A research-based guide for literacy practitioners serving adults with learning disabilities*. Washington, DC: Author.

National Center for Family Literacy. (2005). *Applying research in reading instruction for adults*. Washington, DC: Partnership for Reading (National Institute for Literacy, National Institute of Child Health and Human Development, U.S. Department of Education).

National Institute of Child Health and Human Development (NICHD). (2000). Report of the National Reading Panel. *Teaching children to read: An evidence-based assessment of the scientific research literature on reading and its implications for reading instruction: Reports of the subgroups*. (NIH Publication No. 00-4754). Washington, DC: U.S. Government Printing Office.

Shaywitz, S. (2003). *Overcoming dyslexia*. New York: Knopf, Borzoi, Random House.

Tobias, S. (1995). *Overcoming math anxiety*. New York: W.W. Norton.

Westman, J. C. (1990). Written language disabilities. *Handbook of Learning Disabilities* (pp. 494-513). Needham Heights, MA: Simon & Schuster.

Wolf, M., & Bowers, P. G. (2000). Naming-speed processes and developmental reading disabilities: An introduction to the special issue on the double-deficit hypothesis. *Journal of Learning Disabilities, 33*, 322-324.

Wolf, M., Miller, L., & Donnelly, K. (2000). Retrieval, automaticity, vocabulary, elaboration, orthography (RAVE-O). *Journal of Learning Disabilities, 33*(4), 375-386.

Teacher Resources

Allen, J. (2004). *Tools for teaching content literacy.* Portland, ME: Stenhouse Publishers.

Fry, E. B., Kress, J. E., & Fountoukidis, D. L. (2000). *The reading teacher's book of lists (4th).* Paramus, NJ: Prentice Hall.

Kazemek, F. E., & Rigg, P. (1995). *Enriching our lives: Poetry lessons for adult literacy teachers and tutors.* Newark, DE: International Reading Association.

Kruidenier, J. (2002). *Research-based principles for adult basic education reading instruction.* Washington, DC: National Institute for Literacy.

National Adult Literacy and Learning Disability Center. (1999). *Bridges to practice: A research-based guide for literacy practitioners serving adults with learning disabilities.* Washington, DC: Author.

Web Resources

Assessment Strategies and Reading Profiles – Provides information on instructional strategies and offers a free, online mini-course on teaching reading to adults
http://www.nifl.gov/readingprofiles

Bridges to Practice: Helping Adults with Learning Disabilities – Provides information on how to teach adults with learning disabilities
http://www.nifl.gov/nifl/ld/bridges/bridges.html

LD Online – Provides information and resources on learning disabilities
http://www.ldonline.org

Verizon Literacy Campus – Provides free courses for adult literacy teachers and volunteers
www.literacycampus.org

Index